A "Mischievous Chicken"

By A.K.Kasthuri

With Sanjay R. Srivatsa

ISBN: 978-1-4269-5986-8 (sc)
ISBN: 978-1-4269-5987-5 (e)

Trafford rev. 09/26/2011

 www.trafford.com

North America & international
toll-free: 1 888 232 4444 (USA & Canada)
phone: 250 383 6864 ♦ fax: 812 355 4082

About the Author:

Athur K. Kasthuri is a retired Professor of Geology of Presidency College, Chennai, India. He is an avid collector and paleontologist. He is happily married to Leela and spends his time between Walnut Creek, CA and Chennai, India. This book is the culmination of his lifelong dream to share the mysteries of his life with fellow readers and Baba followers...

Sanjay Srivatsa is married to Prof. Kasthuri's second daughter, Niroop and assisted the Author over a period of 2 years to catalog, transcribe journal notes and render the Author's vivid lifetime experiences into the story of "A Mischievous Chicken".

Front Cover Art: A drawing depicting himself: Avatar Meher Baba

Reminiscences of a fortunate devotee...

The germ of this idea was planted in me by my son-in-law, Daddy-o, my fond name for my grandsons' Vikram and Arjun's Dad. More about Vikram, who opened my eyes to an alternate spiritual paradigm, follows later. I am grateful to my son-in-law, my co-author, who helped me convey all my emotions and thoughts in words and navigate through my lapses of memory.

Two people have influenced me in my life more than anything; one was my Grandfather, the other, is who I write about.

I dedicate this book to my beloved wife Leela, who completes me; my daughters Nirupkanthi and Meherkanthi and my grandchildren Siddharth, Sitara, Vikram and Arjun who continue to inspire me.

A.K.Kasthuri

…..don't worry, be happy…..

Avatar Meher Baba

TABLE OF CONTENTS

CHAPTER One:

THE "AWAKENING"

I can't remember exactly when the concept of God dawned upon me. Many spend a lifetime trying to find an answer to that. The subject is convoluted as there can be several answers…or perhaps there *are* no answers. It is only much later in life that I became aware; the concept is very personal and means different things to different people. There is no one right answer; if you believe in something and mean well, then that is, perhaps the path to its realization. This much I know for sure, in our Hindu faith, the concept of God is thrust upon us very early in childhood. This occurs as we go to temples with our Elders, participate in religious functions or study time immemorial epics that try to portray the presence of the Almighty upon Earth. So, is God the multi-limbed super human, a robed mystic that can perform miracles, or simply a voice from above? These have been several manifestations that we all learn about growing up. Religion tells us God walked amongst us, in times of peril. Does that mean God is one of us? Or…perhaps speaks through one of us? I suppose that explains the root of religion as we have come to understand it. So how do you know when you come across such a person? Is it because, someone tells you so, or because, something is revealed inside you?

Well, quite evidently, I was just as confused as everyone else, growing up. But sometimes you get lucky…and this becomes your guide through life. And so it came to be, sometime during the mid 1930's when I was merely five, that my maternal grandfather, C.V.Sampath Aiyengar, (Grandpa) noting that my sister Vasumathi and I were quite God-fearing, mentioned casually, Meher Baba, was indeed God. He then added "I don't need to repeat this a second time." That was Grandpa…his word was gospel. This austere utterance came shortly after Baba's March 1930 *Darshan*[1] at Saidapet, Madras, (Chennai), where four generations of Grandpa's family came into Baba's fold, and true to Grandpa's vision, we have never looked back. Today in 2010, six generations of our family have been influenced by this spiritual master. Meherwan Sheriar Irani (Meher Baba) was born in a Persian family on Sunday, February 25, 1894, in the City of Poona (Pune), India. There have been many books that detail his life and service. Of special reference is "Lord Meher" – Bhau Kalchuri[2].

Grandpa served in the judicial service of the erstwhile Madras Presidency during British times till his retirement in 1932. In those days, it was quite prestigious to have such a post within the *British Raj*, as the administrative functions were delegated to only well educated and trustworthy Indian professionals. This was a period of quite some turmoil as the British were at war overseas, and desperately, trying to keep control of their colonies. Britain had enjoyed the wealth of its colonies and manpower for centuries and it wasn't about to let go now.

---

1   Viewing/meeting of an enlightened person or deity
2   "The Biography of the Avatar of the Age-Meher Baba", LORD MEHER, 20 volumes by Bhau Kalchuri

To the Crown's dismay, the freedom movement in India in particular, was in full swing, applying great pressure on Her Majesty's dominions. As the pressures of war were mounting, the Queen allowed the civil and judicial administration to permit hiring professionals of Indian origin into Her Majesty's service. So people with special skills were indoctrinated into the civil and judicial system. Grandpa's knowledge of Telugu favored his posting in the Telugu speaking districts of then, the State of Madras, which were later to become part of the State of Andhra Pradesh after India's Independence. Unlike any of his peers, Grandpa was quite progressive and cultivated a cosmopolitan outlook. He conducted his tasks with meticulous adherence to ethics and rules with personal pride. He was well known for his judgments and unflinching adaptation of the tenets of justice. Still, it's possible that he too must have been unsettled as all of us, since his spiritual being was restless.

Grandpa could have been a truth seeker both professionally as well as metaphysically. His spiritual "call" came during 1927 when he realized he had at last found his Master, Meher Baba. I have no record of how Grandpa met Baba or how his initiation began, but Grandpa used to be a voracious reader of theosophical literature and articles. It is perhaps there, that he must have come to witness Baba's movements and growing acceptance. After that, he must have sought him out relentlessly, as was Grandpa's wont, and indoctrinated himself in Baba's mission. Back then, Meher Baba was called "*Sadguru* Meher Baba", literally meaning "everyone's Guru". Baba had already touched many souls in Iran, America and Europe and had engendered quite a following. Dedicating his life to God, Baba had achieved the echelon of a "Spiritual Master" which is perhaps what drew Grandpa to him. Being the first grandson and as such his ward, Grandpa wanted me to accept Baba as soon as

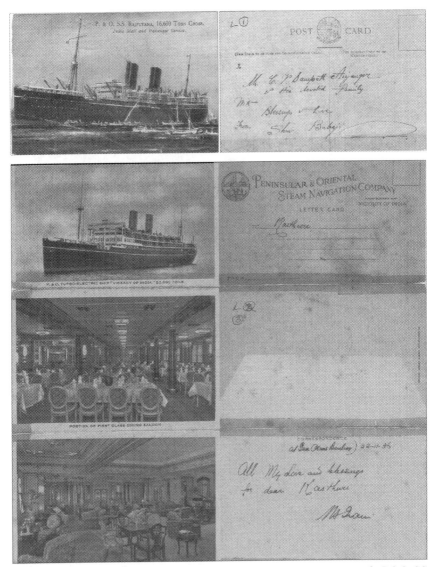

Ref1&2: Letter to Mr. C.V.Sampath Aiyengar - A picture postcard, P&O SS Rajputana & Fold out to Kasthuri

possible. He must have trusted my readiness and his desire to share his discovery being quite paramount, he put me in touch with Baba's *mandali* [3], four of who have had a great influence in my life, since the mid 1930s. They were:

1. Dadachanji (Chanji)[4] Baba's first secretary, and the one who Baba saved from committing suicide,
2. Adi K. Irani or Adi Sr. (Sr. to distinguish him from Adi, Baba's own younger brother) who became Baba's secretary after Chanji, and was based at the trust office at Ahmednagar, Maharastra State,
3. Eruch Jessawala, a constant companion to our Master and his interpreter, and
4. Jal, S Irani or Jal *bhai* (brother Jal), Baba's youngest brother, who endeared himself to the Aiyengars (Grandpas) family since the 1950s.

---

3   Circle of close followers
4   Ref1&2:

Mysore — 20th April 1936

My dear Child — Kasthuri —

I received your Note re:
Your tonsil Operation on Wednesday
It is a petty affair. So - be brave.

Anyway - *I am always*
with You - and have My blessings
as ever - my dear Child.

All My love

M.S.Gram

Ref3: Letter from Baba dated April 30, 1936, on my minor surgery

Grandpa encouraged me to write freely to Baba, as often as possible, cautioning me to never forget that Baba is not just my Elder, but he is God incarnate and thus to be reverential. I have not forgotten this, ever, in my letters or whenever we had his *darshan*. Like a plant quenched with water, my spiritual awareness blossomed and thus began a wonderful and glorious adventure.

As I was quite young, my thoughts and requests were of course childish. I recall my very first communication to Baba, was selfishly, my concern of undergoing a small operation in April of 1936. I received his immediate reply and I nervously opened his comforting and blissful letter from Mysore[5]. Baba's blessings – message was as follows –

Mysore, 20th April 1936

My dear child Kasthuri,

I received your note reg your tonsil operation on Wednesday. It is a petty affair - so be brave.
Anyway I am always with you and you have my blessings as ever–

My Dear Child
All my love
Sd M.S. Irani
(Calligraphy by Chanji)

I guess he was telling me not to worry about such small things in life. Baba sent me a letter card, while travelling by P&O steamship Viceroy of India, (a 5-unit foldout, about this ship) with the following notation, in the handwriting of Chanji,

5   Ref3

At Sea (near Bombay)
22-11-36
All my blessings
For dear Kasthuri
(Sd) M.S. Irani

I began to realize a sense of great accomplishment in writing these letters to someone Grandpa referred to as God, and getting his replies. In short I felt very special. This prompted me to write many more and I continued my letters to Baba from January 1944 onwards, always starting and ending with the words, "our humble prostrations", before signing it. In most cases, the almost immediate replies from the *mandali* – (Adi Sr, Eruch or Jalbhai) have been the only record of my humble letters, stirring in my heart, deep feelings of faith, unending homage and gratitude to my beloved Master.

CHAPTER Two:

LIFE WITH THE ELDERS

I was born at our ancestral home at Saidapet, Madras on September 7, 1925. If my memory serves me right, I spent my early years with my grandparents possibly 1927 through 1932. They were just about my full time guardians.

Beginning service as a district *Munsif* [6] Grandpa traveled a lot in the districts often being coached in horse carriages between the villages. He was so intent in dispensing justice, that he frequently ignored instructions from his superiors to pardon certain defendants who had "extra" influence upon the system in terms of large cash payouts or political clout. These superiors, mostly British nationals and a few senior Indian officials, were obviously not comfortable with his high ethics, especially when he chose to ignore their instructions. Not succeeding with his superiors, the defendants being judged by Grandpa then tried to curry favors, by meeting Grandma with offerings of cash or expensive gifts to persuade Grandpa to judge in their favor. They would also state that this was supported by Grandpa's superiors. Grandma promptly

6   1st ranking official in the judicial department above a *Tasildar*, a revenue official

dispelled them without accepting their offers which displeased Grandpa's judicial higher-ups even more. It was obvious, as they were motivated politically and monetarily, Grandpa's superiors wanted him to go against his better judgment in disposing of criminal cases. In order to show their displeasure and teach him a lesson, even after his promotion as Sub Judge on merit, he was frequently transferred around, while his juniors, who were indiscreet and corrupt, were promoted over him. In addition to playing politics, his superiors were quite conservative and Grandpa's progressive outlook was also a problem among his orthodox colleagues. So it was obvious that when Grandpa was trying very hard to do the right thing, he was tormented at work and he was seeking to find some spiritually comfort in his soul.

His early quest in spirituality peaked when he was a theosophist, an *arya-samajist* [7] and later, a member of the Masonic Lodge, but none of these could satisfy his desire for peace and contentment. His search continued in earnest.

Sometime during 1927 he heard about a saint Babaji (Meher Baba). As the saying goes "when the pupil is ready, the master appears", this is what happened in his case. Upon meeting Baba for the first time, his immediate response was "my heart involuntarily jumped up. I meditated on him, had peace the like of which I never had before – I thought that I became identified with him."

After this meeting his whole outlook on life changed. Very shortly, by a strange coincidence, he was promoted to Principal Sub-Judge in which capacity, he retired after his mandatory service in December 1932. I believe that this promotion was a gift from Baba.

---

7   one of the numerous religious organizations formed by Raja Ram Mohan Roy, which propagated the abolition of Sati – which is self immolation by surviving widows

During the early years with my grandparents, and later at their Bangalore residence in 1933, I was of a sickly disposition due to frequent eye ailments and tonsils. I had also fallen down and sustained a fracture, twice in my right shoulder...but nothing involving surgery or hospitalization. Up to now I had been educated at home with a tutor. My regular schooling commenced in 1933 at Bangalore living with Grandpa, at St Joseph's Indian High School, Bangalore Cantonment. I realize, I spent more of my childhood with my Grandparents than with my own parents. Perhaps this was Grandpa's will as I was his first grandson; or perhaps he had other motivations in light of my spiritual development. Then again, maybe he was trying to protect me in his own way. Compared to the heat of Madras, Bangalore those days was a vacationer's paradise, so I was not complaining anyway.

CHAPTER Three:

"CONTACT"

In the early years of my awakening, I considered Baba as a Mystic, and an ordained spiritual master, but not God incarnate. I cannot explain why I did not see him as the vessel of God until many years into my adulthood. Even when I had to undergo a tonsils operation in 1936 and communicated with Baba in my usual way, it was like approaching an Elder and not one with divine providence. It was only during the summer of 1962, at a place called Guruprasad, Poona (Pune), that I fully realized Baba as a manifestation of God.

Grandpa's contact with Baba found its fulfillment in 1930, when his family had privilege of Baba's *darshan*. Baba's first visit to our ancestral property at Saidapet, Madras took place on March 1 of 1930. This residential property belonged to Grandpa's Father-in-Law and he bequeathed the same for Baba's work, later to be known as "Meher Bhavan". Another property almost opposite this, which was also owned by the family, became "Meher Ashram" and Baba's visit consecrated both these premises. The following extracts from our diaries give the details of this momentous visit.

Ref 4: Baba and Grandpa's family taken March 2, 1930 – (Kasthuri seated on Grandma's lap, 2nd from right)

Ref 5: Baba at Carnatic Studio, taken March 2, 1930

Excerpt from Diary: March 1, 1930: Baba and party had arrived at Sri Perumbudur about forty kilometers south west of Madras. Baba's early disciple, Dastur and Grandpa travelled by car to where Baba and his party were waiting. Baba and Dastur travelled with Grandpa and the rest of the party followed reaching Saidapet around 9 PM on 1st March. Just as the car was turning to go into Brahmin St Saidapet, the location of Meher Bhavan, it stopped suddenly yards from Grandpa's residence. All got down and noticed that one of the front tires of the car fell apart and rolled away. All were shocked but it was understood that it conveyed Baba's mysterious welcome to his home. (Perhaps the car had fulfilled its purpose before breaking down). March 2, 1930: Around 8 Am Baba graced the premises opposite Meher Bhavan and named it Meher Ashram. He planted a sapling of the Peepul Tree to commemorate his visit. Address of welcome to Baba and Dastur was next. Baba visited the nearby harijan[8] colony, went into one of the huts accompanied by Grandpa, my aunt Lakshmi and Dastur. At Meher Bhavan, Baba was pleased to initiate[9] into learning, child Kasthuri, 4 1/2 years old. A group photo with Baba, Grandpas family and other devotees was taken at Meher Ashram, at which time four generations of Grandpa's family came into Baba's fold[10].

A special photo of Baba was also taken at the Carnatic Studios, Madras.
March 3, 1930: Babaji and Dastur left Saidapet in a car and awaited the bus at Poonamalee, a place 20 kilometers south west of Saidapet.

---

8   "Untouchable Caste"
9   Initiation is a very traditional Hindu ceremony to commence the formal learning process
10 Refs 4&5

Grandpa, Aunt Lakshmi and I left Saidapet by bus with Baba's entourage and caught up with Baba at Poonamalee, southwest of Saidapet. With a humble farewell to Baba and his entourage, we returned home. A special feature of Baba's visit was that all of the devotees regardless of castes and creed sat together along with, dear Baba, enjoying the food lovingly prepared by Grandma Kamalammah and Grand Aunt Rajammah. This was my first "contact" with Baba. Being only five years of age, my initial impressions of Baba were perhaps a lot more earthly. I saw him as a peaceful man with a smiling face. But there was a relentless energy in those haunting eyes that forever held me in rapture. I knew right then, this was a very special person.

I am told that a very memorable event occurred shortly after Baba's first visit namely, the opening of a free reading room at "Meher Ashram" on 21st April, 1930. With the help of the acting district collector of Chengulpet, (Saidapet was part of this district at that time) the first publication of the Meher Gazette, a quarterly, was registered on 25th April at Saidapet, sub divisional office. The first issue with a print run of 1000 copies was released on 1st June 1930 containing Baba's blessing to all readers. The Meher Gazette was edited by Aunt Lakshmi, as Grandpa was in service. Being a fair reader by that time, this was my cherished memento and one of my most revered possessions right to this day.

Grandpa and Baba had a very unique unspoken bond and were perhaps linked spiritually. Both reveled in the company of each other and during Grandpa's service at Kurnool, Baba came on a private visit for three days, early in August of 1931, and stayed at Grandpa's cottage there. This was very unusual, since by this time Baba had gone into seclusion and would only avail himself sporadically. So great was his friendship with Grandpa.

These visits were, as I believe now, literally a godsend to me, but at that time, it was simply a chance to be with Baba. I would stick to his every routine and I particularly recollect that Baba had grown a beard which he removed while at Kurnool.

Grandpa was to retire in December 1932 and desired to take a few months leave prior to retirement. Around July 1932, Secretary Chanji, conveyed Baba's suggestion that Grandpa take this opportunity to visit the United Kingdom and Europe and meet a few of his contacts there. After meeting a few of them, his final visit was to be in the Alps. This contact he was to meet, was residing in Switzerland, near a lake resort which was accessible only by a cable car from that resort. Grandpa reached the resort early and as he had time, booked a ride over the Alps to reach Baba's contact. There was only one cable car and only one scheduled trip per day. An hour prior to his ride, Baba's contact appeared as if from nowhere and Grandpa engaged him in a conversation, delivering Baba's felicitations. Both men began discussing theosophy and lost track of time. Finally they bade farewell and parted company. After the contact left, Grandpa realized he did not need to take the cable car ride and went to the ticket booth in an effort to cancel his reservation. But they told him, it was too late as it had already left some time ago. He was about to turn around and leave, when the agent additionally informed him hesitantly, that soon after the cable car had left, it met with an accident enroute and details were awaited. Much later when Grandpa narrated this story to me upon his return, he said beloved Baba had saved his life...again.

After completion of his tour, Grandpa met Baba at Bombay on Feb 3rd, 1933 to fill him in all of the details and convey the respects of his devotees. During this meeting, Baba told Grandpa that he wished to make the Meher

Gazette a bi-monthly publication instead of quarterly. As he had retired and was out of service, Grandpa took over as editor and publisher of the Gazette from my Aunt. The bi-monthly publication commenced with Volume #2, No. 1, effective April 1933.

CHAPTER Four:

EXODUS

On December 3rd 1933, I had the pleasure of greeting Chanji, sent by Baba on his mission, who stayed with us for a few days. During this meeting, Grandpa and the rest of our family begged Chanji to convey to Baba that they would love for him to attend a celebration in honour of his fortieth birthday the next year at "Meher Bhavan". I was giddy with excitement of what was proposed to happen and I would once again have a chance to be with Baba. By then, I was beginning to nurture a special relationship and longed for any chance to be with him. Chanji passed on the message to Baba, and relayed back that Baba would think about their ardent request and invitation. The reason for his unsure response was only appreciated by me much later. Previously, his disciples from Europe, Nonny, Rano Gayly, Ruano Bogislav, had been invited by Baba to come to India for his birthday at his Ashram. They were to travel a long distance for many days just to be with him. I am sure there would also be a lot of local attendees. But now Baba had to choose. So they were cabled not to come to India at this time as Baba was planning his Madras visit on this occasion. I guess he was more drawn to "Meher Bhavan". This once again illustrated the bond between Baba and Grandpa.

Picture taken at the reception accorded to His Holiness Sree Sadguru Meher Baba (garlanded) on arrival at the Madras Central Station Feb. 1934 morning. —P. P. B.

Ref 6: Baba and nine *Mandali*, taken at Central Station, Madras, February, 17, 1934

Author & Sister, Children in forefront

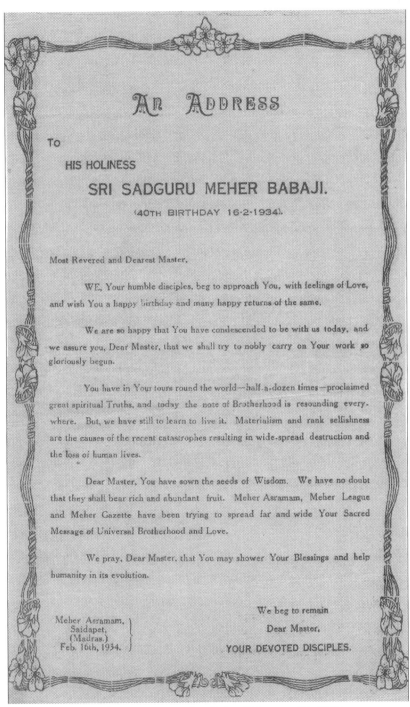

AN ADDRESS

To

HIS HOLINESS

SRI SADGURU MEHER BABAJI.

(40TH BIRTHDAY 16-2-1934).

Most Revered and Dearest Master,

WE, Your humble disciples, beg to approach You, with feelings of Love, and wish You a happy birthday and many happy returns of the same.

We are so happy that You have condescended to be with us today, and we assure you, Dear Master, that we shall try to nobly carry on Your work so gloriously begun.

You have in Your tours round the world—half-a-dozen times—proclaimed great spiritual Truths, and today the note of Brotherhood is resounding everywhere. But, we have still to learn to live it. Materialism and rank selfishness are the causes of the recent catastrophes resulting in wide-spread destruction and the loss of human lives.

Dear Master, You have sown the seeds of Wisdom. We have no doubt that they shall bear rich and abundant fruit. Meher Asramam, Meher League and Meher Gazette have been trying to spread far and wide Your Sacred Message of Universal Brotherhood and Love.

We pray, Dear Master, that You may shower Your Blessings and help humanity in its evolution.

We beg to remain

Dear Master,

Meher Asramam,
Saidapet,
(Madras.)
Feb. 16th, 1934.

YOUR DEVOTED DISCIPLES.

Ref 7: Address of welcome presented to Baba, February 18, 1934

Accepting Grandpa's invite, Baba left Ahmednagar by train February 16th, 1934, reaching Madras Central on the eve of February 17th. By now many other disciples had become aware of Baba's visit. Grandpa and other disciples received Baba with great joy and revelry at the station. Baba had come with nine of his *mandali*. A group photo of Baba and his disciples was taken before they left for Meher Bhavan[11].

On arrival, *aarathi*[12] was performed welcoming our Master. Baba stayed with us till the morning of 19th February. I still remember it like yesterday. His fortieth birthday was celebrated on the 18th at Meher Ashram with *aarathi*, prayers and *Bhajans*[13]. An address of welcome was presented[14]. Two group photos were taken on this occasion[15]. More photos of Baba were taken, and Baba lovingly yielded to the request of my Aunt and Mother Janaky to dress as Lord Shiva and Lord Krishna. A large public meeting was held in the evening. A special message dictated by Baba was read out by one of his *mandali*, Rustom. While I could not spend a lot of personal time with Baba, just watching all the devotees swarm around him and the general feeling of goodwill began to instill Baba's mission in my mind. I couldn't explain it then, but I was slowly coming under the spell of Baba's message of love. After prayers at Meher Ashram on the morning of the 19th, Baba left for Meherabad with his entourage.

---

11   Ref 6,
12   Hindu ritual of welcoming auspicious guests using lit camphor, flowers and sandalwood paste
13   Hindu spiritual songs
14   Ref 7
15   Ref 8,9

Ref 8: Baba at Meher Ashram, Saidapet, Madras, taken February 18,1934

Later that year, Grandpa purchased a house in Bangalore in an area called Shankarapuram and named it "Kamala Bhavan". By this time Grandpa had very much taken charge of his grandchildren's development and felt that his decisions were in our best interest to grow scholastically and spiritually. Maybe, he did not want that influence to wane, or be displaced, so without much ado, when he moved to Bangalore, he took Grandma, me and my sister with him. Only much later in my life did I come to recognize the true import of our relocation. It was an exodus that Grandpa had designed for me, so as not to be subjugated by influences in our ancestral home and put my mind with verve on the path of realization. Of course, I did not have any qualms about this since I had grown to respect and enjoy being with Grandpa....and of course, where there is Grandpa, there would be Baba!

Just as I had expected, my wishes were rewarded within a year, as Baba with four of his *mandali*, arrived by train from Poona to Bangalore on 18th April 1934. He surprised Grandpa who received him at the station by saying "we will go to your house for the night". Though unprepared, Grandpa was very happy, exclaiming, "It is my family's great good luck." Arriving at "Kamala Bhavan" that night our joy knew no bounds. Arrangements for a comfortable stay were devotedly made by Grandma for Baba and his party. Baba noticed I was there and gave me and my sister a special hug. They were all served food and talked late into the night.

During this trip Baba and Grandpa made several visits to nearby cities to meet other devotees. I particularly remember an event that is still fresh in my mind as told by my Aunt. On the 27th Baba and his entourage left for Kengeri, a nearby village enroute to Mysore. Three days later, my Aunt who had come to visit Baba, took Grandpa's car with a driver to Kengeri, to bring back Baba and party to Bangalore. On the way back, the narrow road outside the city had become quite busy and traffic was heavy with trucks, carts and animals crossing. While trying to pass a bullock cart, Grandpa's car literally ran into a herd of cows. A few cows that were hit just scampered away unhurt while one calf was run over and was lying lifeless on the road. In fear of retribution and getting beaten by the mob that was now forming, the driver got out of the car and promptly sneaked away. My Aunt was badly shaken by the accident and the plight of the slain calf. Baba consoled her saying, "it is alright. The calf was lucky to be run over with me here. Do not be afraid." Then, they all got down and approached the totally still creature on the road. Baba bent down and gently touched the calf upon its head. The calf stirred at first, opened its doleful eyes, sniffed his hand and to everybody's relief, immediately got up and bounded away looking quite unhurt! As everyone watched, mesmerized, the calf joined its mother, mooing loudly, and even the unruly mob cheered at the miracle that had just ensued. Joyfully, my Aunt and the rest of the party got back in the car only to find that their driver had repaired back, sensing that he was safe from the now jubilant crowd. He soon took the wheels and drove the party back to "Kamala Bhavan". When I heard that story, and even now, I sometimes ponder the significance of the event. Karma guides our actions and deeds as well as the outcome. Every living being experiences karma ...and so did the calf, that opportune day.

CHAPTER Five:

BABA, MY PLAYMATE

Since Grandpa purchased "Kamala Bhavan" in Bangalore early 1933 and we moved there, I remained with my Grandparents all the time. My regular schooling commenced at Bangalore later that year. I was admitted for a year at Kamalabai School at Bangalore Cantonment which was co-educational up to Grade V. The Cantonment area was so designated by the British for maintaining a military zone at some distance from Bangalore city, ruled by the Maharaja of Mysore. It was similar to a garrison city. My Aunt also remained with us after her first visit and had already taken over as the first headmistress at this school. I completed two years at this school without incident. It was interesting and strange to see my Aunt at home and at school as the headmistress. Later with Grandpa's influence, I got admitted in Form II (Grade VII) at St Joseph's Indian High School also in the Cantonment area. During those times educational institutions in the Cantonment area were under the jurisdiction of the Director of Public Instruction, Madras (State). Being under ten, I was found to be a few months underage for admission. The school principal, Reverend Father C. Browne, solved this problem when he suggested to Grandpa to simply have my birth month on file changed from September to January of the same year, 1925. It was possible to do such things back then if you knew the right people. School education under this system was for eleven years namely, classes one through five, followed by forms one through six. I completed my Fourth Form (Grade IX) at St Joseph's in the summer of 1937.

Meanwhile, Baba had acquired two residences in Bangalore, one at the Links, and the other at Palace Road, within the Cantonment area. When Grandpa finally shifted the family to back Saidapet, Madras to retire in his ancestral home in 1937, "Kamala Bhavan" was retained and taken care of, and Baba remained in Bangalore till 1940 at his residences.

A significant event took place at "Kamala Bhavan" during one of many Baba's visits and stay there. On one occasion, I recall Chanji was also with Baba. Baba had sent Grandpa on some errand away from the house. Grandma was attending to Baba and Chanji's needs. When lunch was ready she kindly requested them to come for lunch. As Baba wanted to rest, he asked Grandma to serve lunch to Chanji and suggested he would eat later. Chanji was puzzled with this arrangement. Then, when Baba suggested my sister and I come upstairs to him, Chanji was really perturbed. He wanted to make sure that Baba did not miss his meal. Chanji protested, but Baba got his way and made Chanji go for lunch. True to Grandpa's training we never questioned, been disrespectful to Baba or forced ourselves on him. When he called us upstairs, little did we know that we were about to see, yet another side of Baba – our playmate.

A brief mention of Kamala Bhavan: It had a very spacious downstairs with two separate wings and a large hall between them. A staircase in the hall led upstairs. It opened into a midsized corridor with a room on either side

Refs 10, 11: With Baba, Jal, Chanji, Gustadji, taken in Bangalore, February 16, 1936,

matching the plinth below. Baba's room was on the left and Grandpa's was on the right. Baba's room had an *almirah*,[16] a chair and a cot.

This is where we found out about Baba's playful inclinations. Baba wanted us to take part in games with him, which was a totally enthralling experience. Up until now, we were only witness to Baba, the seer, the prophet, and the revered, but this experience revealed the playful child in him. He played three games with us. The first game was hide and seek: – Baba would hide within the room when we had our eyes closed. Shortly we had to open our eyes and find him when he clapped. Regardless of how small the room was, we had a tough time locating his hiding place. It was like now we see him, now we don't. I really thought that he was making himself invisible, the yogi that he was! We could only find him after he clapped and revealed his hiding place, in spots where the two of us had looked already. Next it was our turn to hide but we were no competition for him.

The second game was sudden motion, stop and go: - Asking us to each hold one of his hands he suddenly moved forwards with a jerk, leaving us stranded. Next while walking with us, he would halt suddenly, leaving us pitching forward. Baba's smile at this time was magical. The game left all of us laughing to our hearts content and we slowly realized he had become one of us...a playmate! The third game was long finger trick: – Baba would make a steeple with his fingers from one hand and enclose the "steepled" fingers with his other hand, exposing only the tips of the "steepled" fingers. Then we would take turns to try and find his long finger and pinch on it. When he exposed his closed fingers, invariably we had always chosen the wrong finger! At times, when we were right on target, he would jerk his hand like he slipped, and his jerk would make us land on an incorrect finger. Then we would both yell at him and have

16   Free standing cupboard

a good laugh! I had read that Baba played this trick with kids on many occasions but for us it was a special treat that we would cherish for the rest of our lives. I could not understand the special significance of this event. When Baba got tired, we went down and found Grandpa and told him of the games Baba played with us, but there was no reaction from him, only surprise. Perhaps, we had experienced something that Grandpa could never have...

An important event, foretold by Baba, took place on 4th January 1936, at Bangalore. Baba requested his devotees all over the world, not to celebrate his 42nd birthday, as he would be in seclusion. On Sunday, 16th February 1936, his birthday as per Zoroastrian calendar, Baba was at Grandpa's house at "Kamala Bhavan" on a private visit. He was accompanied by brother Jal, Chanji and Gustadji who also stayed at Grandpa's residence. As per Baba's wishes, no *Aarthis* or worship was performed. For some reason that I cannot recall, he started a discussion, where the various members of the household presented various concerns and problems in their life. I found it fascinating to watch him as he courteously listened to each person, and quickly resolved their concerns with a few selected words, overwhelming all that were present. The basic tenet of his message was that love conquers all. If one focuses on that, most problems seem trivial. So great was the significance of this simple event that Grandpa remarked: "we have received the highest boon on Baba's birthday with a chance of experiencing his love for us all".

A family photo[17] with Baba, Jal, Chanji and Gustadji was taken as also one of Baba alone – precious mementos for all of us.

---

17   Ref 10, 11

As I began comprehending Baba as a true seer of events, I learnt about another important incident, which Baba had foretold, that took place at Khushroo Quarters, Ahmednagar that day. Upasni Maharaj who was a very well respected spiritual guide in his own right, unexpectedly arrived there from Sakori, after a lapse of fifteen years. He stood before Meher Baba's photo in the room, and uttered prayers with folded hands for about five minutes. He also performed Baba's *Aarthi* and instructed Adi Sr and his Mother Gulmai, to convey this information to Baba.

Baba was again at "Kamala Bhavan", Bangalore, on a visit with Chanji, Pendu and Norina Matchabelli, his devotees from USA. He said at that time, "the *avatar*[18] does not tread even a single lane, without considering its worth." This was on 24ᵗʰ January 1936, before he even knew about Upasni Maharaj's visit. Such were the small incidents and revelations that wove into the fabric of my growing realization that Baba was much more than a Spiritual Master.

As I had mentioned earlier, we had shifted from Bangalore to our ancestral home in 1937. Grandpa was at Bangalore again on 8ᵗʰ September 1939, when Baba had called for a meeting to discuss his plan for a universal spiritual center at Byramangala, off Bidadi railway station on the Bangalore-Mysore route. Proposals for this were being finalized which needed his presence. Grandpa's task was to plan the inauguration of the center, which the Divan of Mysore, Sir Mirza Ismail was to attend as the guest of honour. It was decided to have the ceremony at Byramangala. Baba's message on this occasion was read out by Grandpa. Speeches were later delivered by Aunt and others. I was not present at this event, but relate this as it was told to me by my Aunt.

18   Celestial reincarnation

A few *Parsis*[19] including some relatives of Baba, who were antagonistic to him, were spreading rumours about him. A relative with the same name as Baba, a Lt Col M.S.Irani, who was spreading false propaganda, produced copies of a pamphlet, "The Spiritual Hoax of M.S.Irani". These pamphlets were arranged to be distributed at the foundation ceremony to disrupt the proceedings. The pamphlets were being rushed over to the location of the proceedings by van. By some strange quirk of fate, on the way to Byramangala, the van lost control due to speeding and capsized, but without any harm to the occupants. The van was unavoidably delayed, and naturally, the pamphlets never reached their destination. When I heard about this recount, I was at first troubled why Baba would have people antagonistic to him, especially his relatives. But then hasn't history taught us that the people closest to you may be the ones who really do not understand you? I will never know what motivated his relatives or why the accident occurred which thwarted their mission of hate, but I find it hard to ignore the fact that Baba was perhaps aware of this...he was the true seer.

---

19   Refugees of Persia

CHAPTER Six:

MANTLE OF RESPONSIBILITY

By now the wonder years were behind me and I had to take my station in life. But to describe the events that led to my coming of age, I go back to the period when we shifted from "Kamala Bhavan", Bangalore to "Meher Bhavan", Madras in the summer of 1937. Even after the relocation, there were occasional trips I made to Bangalore with Grandpa, either when Baba was at Bangalore or during our holidays. Due to the higher elevation, Bangalore had become quite a haven during the hot and unbearable summer months in Madras. Summer in Bangalore as I remember was still very cool, with the Bougainvilleas and "Gulmohar" (flame of the forest) trees in full blossom. The metro areas abounded with parks and gardens and I took great pleasure in returning there to take long walks with Grandpa on the aromatic Bangalore city avenues. Grandpa returned to Bangalore many times to be with Baba till 1940, often to discuss about the Meher Gazette as he was still its chief editor until the very last issue in 1938. When he was in Madras, his main focus was to get me and my sister admitted in a good school so we could continue our education without losing ground. At that time, Annie Besant, an English matron, had established a theosophical school that showed no distinction between caste and creed. All religions were welcome here. Being right in line with his philosophy, Grandpa used his influence to get my sister and me admitted at the famous Besant Theosophical High School, during the summer of 1937 in the hope of continuing to nurture his vision in us. I joined the Fifth Form (Grade X) at this school in a class twenty strong. The fifth and sixth form studies required taking an optional subject such as Physics, Chemistry or History. Out of the twenty, only two of us opted for Physics. The largest section opted for Chemistry. At that time there was only one Science teacher, Mr. Felix Leighton, who could teach but one class; i.e., the Chemistry students, leaving the two Physics students to fend for ourselves for the entire year. Thus we were un-coached and unsupervised in both the theory and practical.

At first it seemed rather fun that we could supervise ourselves, but in reality, being boys, we spent more time day dreaming, so obviously this became a problem for us. Further, even with a good teacher, Physics is a tough subject. When Grandpa saw my poor grade, he was livid. When I told him the reason, he would have none of it, so he pulled me out of this famous school by the end of the school year. He got me admitted for my Sixth Form (Grade XI) at a nearby Ramakrishna Mission Boys High School. But my problems were not over. I was still very weak in Physics as I had lost an entire year of proper coaching. To cover up for this, he arranged for a home tutor from my new school. Initially, I was a bit unsettled being moved about from school to school each year, but only much later did I come to appreciate Grandpa's commitment to my education. Getting proper schooling and a tutor at home helped me pass the Secondary School Board Exam (SSLC) with distinction. All along through my schooling, as also later, Grandpa's involvement in my studies was very evident. Wherever the texts furnished were in the regional language, Grandpa managed to get me parallel sets of texts in English which were quite hard to get and prepared notes for me wherever needed. So great was his dedication to my future that I began seeing him as my mother, father and spiritual guide.

All this time, Baba was at Bangalore during 1939 and 1940. One day, after one of his favorite disciples Nonny's demise in October of '39, Baba remarked, "Before the Big War ends two of the circle will pass away ..." While I had heard of this, I did not grasp the importance of this utterance until much later...

In those days, after 11 years of formal schooling and prior to entering a college, every student had to take a two year course called Intermediate. This was solely to prepare the student for College and help them decide which line of specialization they would be seeking for higher education. High school education over, I was admitted to the well known Pachayappa's College where Grandpa's good friend Prof. D.S.Sharma was the Principal. The courses of study involved English, Tamil and three optional subjects. My choice was Physics, Chemistry and Logic. I was not good in Math and did not opt for Natural Sciences as it required the study of zoology. This meant that for the practical lab sessions I would have to dissect frogs and insects. I could not even bring myself to think about this. As many children raised in the Hindu faith, I was a pure vegetarian and loathed dealing with dead insects and reptiles.

If Grandpa was the architect of my early education, I felt that Baba was the Engineer. Whenever I was faced with any problem I would meditate upon his name, and just as I had seen him dispel everyone's concerns... my obstacles seemed to just evaporate away. This was evident when after few days into college, I saw on the notice board, an invitation for applications for merit scholarships. The program awarded a full course fee waiver based on two written papers in General Knowledge and

English. Unfortunately, when I got wind of it, it was also the final day for applicants. Summoning Baba's grace, I put an application for the merit exam to be held the following week. For some reason, I did not inform Grandpa about this. Perhaps I did not want him to get excited. The results were announced a month later. As I stood dazed in front of the bulletin board, I looked on the circular posted to see if I had made it. There towards the middle of the list was Kasthuri, A.K. I was one of twenty students who qualified for the scholarship for a period of two years! Brimming with excitement, I now conveyed this news to Grandpa and the Elders at home. When the college fees paid during admission were refunded, I handed over the check to Grandpa. After a warm hug from him, he made use of the amount to get me what was known as Faraday's game box of Science, a set of three boxes that I cherished for many years. So great was my faith in Baba, I could simply contemplate on his being, and that would give me the motivation to be successful.

I can recall with amazement, the various ways Grandpa encouraged me to also expand my horizons, by actively pursuing hobbies like philately, numismatics, photography and reading. His gift of stamps and coins to me after his visit to Europe was the initiation into such activities as well as my growing interest in astronomy, solving puzzles, and quizzes.

As had become my steadfast routine, before entering my second year of the intermediate course (1940 – 1941), I wrote to beloved Baba after my 1st year exams. Not that I did not work hard studying for the course material, but these letters to Baba were a great source of comfort and motivation. I would spend hours drafting and redrafting these letters and then be on pins and needles checking the mail everyday for a hopeful response. Of course he never let me down. As in this case, his gracious reply was[20]:

---

20   Ref 12

Bangalore.
13.3.40.

Dear Kasthuri,

Shri Baba has received your loving letter and has asked me write to you how happy he was to read it. He blesses you & wants you not to worry about anything but to answer your papers with full confidence.

With love & blessings of Shri Baba for you all.

yours sincerely,
Jal Kerawalla

Ref 12: Letter from Baba, March 13, 1940 on my appearance for Intermediate exams

Bangalore 13-3-1940

Dear Kasthuri,

Shri Baba has received your loving letter and has asked me to write to you how happy he was to read it. He blesses you and wants you not to worry about anything, but to answer your papers with full confidence.

With love and blessings of Shri Baba for you all.

Yours Sincerely

(sd) M.S.Irani (sd) Jal Kerawala

Baba's blessings and Grandpa's guidance helped me in completing the intermediate course in the summer of 1941, with a 1st Class and distinctions in all the three electives.

Now with college preparatory behind me, I was ready for entry to undergraduate studies. Due to my interest in physical sciences and proficiency demonstrated in Intermediate studies, Grandpa advised me to pursue undergraduate studies in this very field. Thus, I applied for admission to Chemistry, BSc Honours, a three year course, at Presidency College, Madras in the summer of '41. I was thoroughly overjoyed when I received my admission card for the course. At this juncture, my Aunt told me that Grandpa, on Baba's advice about my future, suggested I opt for a course in Geology at the same institution. Up until this time, I had never been exposed to this field of study, nor had any opportunity to know for myself whether I would be successful in this line. But as always, I yielded to Grandpa and Baba as they had the ability of knowing what was best for me. I looked upon it as an opportunity to learn something completely new. While India has had a rich tapestry of physical sciences dating back beyond the Egyptian civilization, the formal documentation of this rich heritage was just at its inception. This presented endless possibilities in its field of education and practice. But the field of Geology was very new within the educational institutions in India and I did not know if it was being offered or even if there were any seats available. Yet again I reminded myself, that if it was ordained by Baba, it would be a reality. As it happened, Presidency College had initiated a course on Geology in 1910, with particularly an Honours program. In 1941, for the first time in the history of the College, a record number of students applied as it was one of the most sought after courses that year. Only twelve students were admitted that July...by Baba's grace, one of them was me.

While I was voraciously consuming the lectures offered that quarter, an event of global significance took place on December 7, 1941. We learnt about this only in the subsequent weeks... after the sneak attack of Japanese warships and "*Kat`e*" torpedo planes, on Pearl Harbor, USA, this "day in infamy" propelled in earnest the onslaught of World War II. This would have its impact, albeit in a small way upon me.

The first year university exams in English Preliminary got over in March 1942. With Baba's blessings I was one of only two of the twelve passing this exam. Throughout the year, we heard about the war in Europe and Southeast Asia on the radio and news articles. As a student in India at that time, one may not have comprehend the magnitude and impact of this event. But even in a small way, I feel that it was Baba's beckoning, that motivated me to contribute to the war effort. Since the British were allies with the American forces and as India was under British rule, educational institutions had to arrange for exhibitions as a measure of raising funds for the war effort. One such was held at the Island Grounds in Madras in December 1942, whereupon our Geology Department put up a stall displaying specimens of rocks and other material. Donations were collected towards the war effort throughout the week. The display and discussions were a hit; large crowds gathered and donated abundantly.

Meanwhile, at a national level, the desire for freedom from British rule was drawing a large number of students to join parties demanding independence from the Crown. This move was strengthened when our national leaders were arrested and thrown in prison for practicing *Satyagraha*[21]. A tragic turn took place when the Secretary to Mahatma Gandhi, one Mahadev Desai, died during this imprisonment. I remember the outcry at the student level which intensified student agitations. Our college principal, an Englishman named H.C.Papworth, boldly declared a holiday for our college in 1943, in honour of the slain freedom fighter. When the British government got wind of this, and considering this an affront to their presence in India, they promptly dismissed Mr. Papworth from service. No one expected this outcome, nor did I like to see Principal Papworth unfairly removed. I recall that there were moments that I meditated upon Baba to glean the reason for this twist of fate. Strangely, the incident had some significance despite its sombre effect. Since there were no qualified British personnel available, ironically, this led to the appointment of the first Indian principal for Presidency College, who was a senior Professor of Chemistry in this institution. In my mind, this tolled the first bells of the end of British rule in India.

I completed my 2nd year Honours course during summer of '43. Before entering the final year of the course in July, Grandpa passed away on 20th

21   Non-violent aggression

June 1943 ... he was only sixty six. Grandma was at Bangalore during this time and returned the next day when we informed her about this. I was devastated. It was like a part of me had broken and gone away. I struggled to keep calm, but inside was a tidal wave of sorrow that quite engulfed me. I ran across the house into "Meher Ashram" and wept like a child. After I was emotionally spent, a strange calm took over me. It was almost like Baba was sitting at the tree and speaking, "Live the legacy" again and again. I realized at that moment, I had to be the Man now and needed to be strong for the family. Upon returning, my Mother and I informed Baba about Grandpa's demise by telegram. Baba sent the following reply telegram

STOP AIYENGAR HAS JOINED ME IN INFINITY STOP

At that moment I knew that I would continue receiving guidance as the two souls had become one.

Later, we learnt that Chanji had passed away in 1944, while he was doing Baba's work in Kashmir. Soon after that, Adi Sr., Baba's assistant, came to Madras on Baba's mission, asking permission to stay at "Meher Bhavan". That night, he reminded us that Baba's oracle had revealed itself. This was the mysterious reference that Baba had made in Bangalore in 1939 when he foretold… "Two of my circle, will not survive the great war…"And thus it came to pass.

I finished my final exams in March 1944 and being the oldest child it was necessary now, for me to take on the mantle of my family's financial strains. No sooner than the results were announced in July, I was ready for employment. I had passed with distinction and had seen through Grandpa's Legacy and sadly, the end of a great patriarch. I now knew the real meaning of his message and principles.

CHAPTER Seven:

THIRST FOR KNOWLEDGE

After graduating with a BSc Honours in Geology, I was consumed with the idea of becoming a Geology Professor. This would allow me to continue increasing my knowledge in this field, while being able to support our joint family. However, my professor had confided in me and my Aunt that there was no vacancy on his staff as the only available teaching assistant post was already filled. He suggested I should study Law and put in an application to Law College as there was a great future in that field in our burgeoning republic. Taking his advice, I got admission into Law College which at that time worked in two shifts. It was early July, 1944. This was a very peculiar digression in my career path particularly as Baba's suggestion that I take up Geology, echoed in my Aunt's mind. When she told me of this, I said "our faith and conviction in Baba remain absolute and all of us are resigned to his will. If it is to be…we will know." I had trained to be in Science, and yet, here I was studying Law which put me quite out of sorts. Early in August, when I had finished about a month's study at Law College, I received information from my professor at Presidency College asking me to meet him the next day in his office. I was quite perplexed with this request; nevertheless, I went to see him. Upon meeting him at an appropriate time, he presented me with an application for the post of an Additional Teaching Assistant. This job had never existed before and such a newly sanctioned post during war times was highly significant. He asked me if I was still interested in the position or if I was now seduced by the glitter of a legal profession. I could only attribute this change of fate to Baba's grace and I could feel his words pouring out of my mouth…"I'll take it!" My professor took me to the Principal right away and confirmed my posting in the Geology Department. Baba may "speak" in mysterious ways, but his bounty is surely intended for the people who have faith in him.

I had accepted my new job with such fervor that I had completely forgotten fees were already paid for my Law College course. These were of course non-refundable and there were educational expenses for my younger brother and sister. So funds were needed in a hurry and I was the only one who could furnish it. There was some time before I had to report for duty which was on 14th August, 1944. I also had to procure appropriate clothing for my new appointment. Due to the war, there was government rationing of clothing and provisions at that time, but quite unexpectedly, an unsolicited friend was able to help me in getting proper clothing material for my posting. This helped me remain frugal as Grandpa had taught us and thus began my contributory phase to the family at "Meher Bhavan" and to the advancement of Geology.

King's Road
Ahmednagar
6-12-44

My dear Kasthuri,

Shri Baba
received your letter. He received
letters of Meher, Srimathi & Jayanthi.
He was pleased & happy to read
them. He was very happy that
Srimathi stood first. and Meher
did so well in three subjects. Little
Jayanthy's letter was so sweet. Baba
liked it the most. Give them all
Babas sweet love and blessings.
Baba is satisfied
with your work. He is happy you
like it. Your love for him will
make you recipient of his grace.
He sends you his blessings.

Yours brotherly
Adi

Ref 13: Letter from Baba, December 6, 1944 on my first employment

As I recall even now, I remembered Baba's saying: "Any person in any difficulty at any time, if he thinks of me wholeheartedly, the difficulty will be resolved." He then reinforced that by saying: "I give you the inner strength to confront the difficulty, face it and overcome it."

My job enabled me to use this as a learning experience, dealing with young minds and interacting with my senior colleagues. A few months into my job, I felt it appropriate to offer my respects and write to Baba about my work. In reply, I received the following letter from Baba's Secretary, Adi Sr.[22] who conveyed Baba's responses from his slate pad:

Kings Road,
Ahmednagar
6-12-1944

My dear Kasthuri,

Shri Baba received your letter. Baba is satisfied with your work. He is happy you like it. Your love for him will make you recipient of his grace. He sends you his blessings.

Yours Brotherly Adi

During summer of 1945, I received a promotion under emergency rules, due to the lack of service commission candidates, to the post of Assistant Professor of Geology. This was a temporary post renewed as needed, each year. I was only 19 years old then. The number of students in Geology had increased with twenty four students in BSc and twelve in BSc Honours. I had requested my professor to allot in my timetable at least one hour for each of the classes I was to teach. This would give me an opportunity to teach various branches of Geology according to the curriculum for each

22   Ref 13

year. This was promptly approved. I diligently prepared for the theory and practical classes and maintained a record of material covered during each working day. During this period and up to the early '50s, the staff was not required to fill a time sheet, and yet all my colleagues worked as a team for six days every week, diligently. That was the dedication of the teachers. I too, followed this strict regimen, as in my case the posting was only temporary and would be repealed at any time. Soon that year, the State Service Commission called for applicants from various subjects to be interviewed for regular (tenured) appointment as Assistant Professors. To my utter joy and fulfillment, I was regularized for this post from the summer of '46. So now I was a tenured professor in the Presidency College Madras which was the only institution offering a Geology degree. I knew now, what Grandpa had labored to instill in me and the future that Baba had divined for me.

At Presidency College, Geology students were involved in field trips and mapping terrains during their course. I was privileged to take them on two or three field trips every year. Back then, these journeys seemed like a pioneering adventure. We camped near villages often using bullock carts for the field equipment such as *Theodolites, Brunton Compass*[23], hammers, chisels, as well as provisions and cooking equipment. The field studies involved hiking six to ten miles each day before moving to another site. Many of these trips were in remote areas with little infrastructure and security. It wasn't just the fact that we had a lot of expensive gear with us, but I was actually responsible for the lives and safety of the young students. So before each tour I always wrote to Baba, seeking his blessings so that we may have a fruitful field trip and return safely. All the field trips over the years of my service, while exciting and educationally stimulating, passed without any disruptive incidents to my great relief.

---

23   Geological Survey equipment

CHAPTER Eight:

GRANDPA'S LEGACY

I feel it was by Baba's design that I spent my early life and formative years with Grandpa. This was from 1929 or so when Grandpa was in service and from 1933 at "Kamala Bhavan", Bangalore, till about the end of my schooling. In between, there were short stays at our ancestral home at "Meher Bhavan".

Grandpa was born in 1877. He had two daughters, the eldest Aunt Lakshmi, born 1904 and my mother, Janaky, born 1909. Other family members at home were Grandpa's cousin, Ramanujam, my Grandma, Kamalammah, her sister Rajammah as also Grandma's parents, Raghavacharlu and his wife Papammah. As was typical at that time, the three generations lived as a joint family.

Child marriages were the norm in those days. Such was the case when my Aunt was married at around age ten. After the ceremony, as was the tradition, she stayed with her parents at home until she came of age before joining her husband. As atrocious as this may sound, many families practiced this to actually preserve the future of their daughters. Being primarily a male dominated society, an unmarried daughter of late age was an undesirable situation for both the parents as well as the daughter. Both could be disparaged by the society. There was always this tremendous burden that a parent felt, which would keep mounting until they were able to give the daughter away in marriage. In fact, when friends came to visit new born baby girls, instead of congratulating the parents, they have often been quoted saying, "so sorry...it is a girl." One has to immerse in this mindset and rigid societal belief to understand that perhaps this is why child marriages were permitted and practiced by the parents of little girls. Unfortunately, there was still no guarantee that the marriages were sustainable.

As in my Aunt's case, suddenly and quite before she came of age, her husband died after an illness leaving her a child widow. At that time, for a young woman, much less a mere child, there was no fate worse than becoming a widow. Her life would be snuffed like a doused candle flame...even before it started. Before the child knew why, she would forever be, ostracized from society, from temples and from other people's homes, lest they befall the same fate. Literally, the future for that child, as she knew it, would end. The parents would not support the child into adulthood, especially if they had other siblings with prospects of marriage, as a widow in the family was considered a bad omen. No wonder *sati*[24] was permitted.

However, undaunted by the calamity that befell his young daughter, and spurning all conventional practices, Grandpa dispelled the event like it never happened. Even as he was ostracized by his orthodox relatives and community, he supported and encouraged my Aunt to complete her schooling all the way to post-graduate study in History. She later also

24   Death of a widowed wife by self immolation

obtained a degree in teaching. Grandpa's foresight and initiative enabled her to be a pioneer in the field of education and participate in social work. She was to be a great help to our family later on.

Either due to her traumatic experience or for some other reason, my Aunt decided to remain a spinster. So Grandpa began seeking an alliance for his younger daughter, my mother, who was fourteen at that time. On the suggestion of a family friend, an eligible groom, born in 1897 to a respectable family of Hyderabad, was sought as an appropriate alliance based on family lineage and horoscopic charts. The wedding of Janaky with Krishnaswamy, my father, ensued shortly thereafter in 1923. I was born when my mother was sixteen and my father was twenty-eight. All of us continued to live in our ancestral home at Grandpa's request.

Surely by this point, one would find it odd that I don't make much reference to my own Father. Sadly there was not much I could refer to. Strange as it may seem, my relationship with Father never took root. Father was a graduate and did his pre-medical courses at Hyderabad. Soon after me, my sister, Vasumathi, was born in 1927. Father was interested in getting a medical degree and had secured admission in the FRCS[25] program at Dublin University, Ireland. This was a very prestigious course in an equally prestigious institution. But he did not get any scholarship for this course and the fees as well as living expenses were quite unaffordable. His elder brother, a leading advocate at Secunderabad, (Hyderabad's twin city), and his only relative capable of funding him did not support my father's wishes to study abroad without aid. But Grandpa would not have it any other way. Impressed by my father's desire to advance in his career; Grandpa managed to obtain a conditional loan from the *Nizam's*[26] government,

25   Fellow of the Royal College of Surgeons
26   Local Royalty

towards father's study abroad. Not only would he now have a doctor for a Son-in-Law, but he was also fulfilling Father's dream.

So Father left for Dublin, late 1927, when I was merely two years old. I now feel that Grandpa took this opportunity to suggest to Mother that I should live with him and Grandma so Mother could take proper care of my baby sister, born May 1927. This started my lifelong affiliation with Grandpa, who took his role as my mentor and parent. Two years transpired and by a peculiar turn of events, Father came back from Dublin rather abruptly and unannounced, obtaining only a Licentiate in Medicine (L.M.Dublin) which was not a fully fledged MD degree. This was a major blow to Grandpa's dream of his Son-in law returning with a prestigious FRCS Doctorate degree. Added to this agony, the "Study Loan" Grandpa had taken became due immediately and had to be repaid in full, as the conditions of the loan were not fulfilled by qualifying for the FRCS. Mother told me later, that Grandpa was livid but did not show it. It was perhaps at that time that Grandpa lost all confidence in my father as a responsible person and someone who could be counted on. To my father's defense, I learnt much later that he found the cold, wet climate quite unsuitable for him to stay any longer. Perhaps there were other reasons that I did not know of, but I did not try to find out. For Grandpa, his misfortunes seemed to come in waves, Aunt becoming a child widow, Father coming back without his MD degree and now the immediate repayment of Father's loan. Although I have little recollection of the matter, I can surmise the stress created in his relationship with Grandpa. It must have been quite intense and this tension must have continued to grow and fester.

Adding fuel to fire, Father was indifferent to Baba. This is natural as he did not grow up under Baba's influence, and soon after his marriage he went to Dublin. I became aware of this during Baba's visits to Saidapet, when my father was not there to receive him, participate in his *Darshan,* or appear in any of the group pictures. I suspected that he did not subscribe to Baba or share the same feelings as we all did. This was later confirmed in 1933, when my mother informed me that Father was not convinced about Baba's spirituality. Perhaps Grandpa was aware of this and was allowing Father the time to understand and finally accept Baba as his savior. Nevertheless, this must have added more distance in their relationship. Hinduism preaches us to consider all religions as one and let our heart lead us to recognize God or the Messiah. We were also truly a multi-faith reverent family. But it must have been hard for someone like Grandpa, who was so devoted to Baba, to come to terms that someone within his own fold was a doubter.

During these years, our family grew and we were blessed with the arrival of my brother, who was named "Mehernath" (literally, lover of Baba), and my sisters Srimathy in 1932 and Jayanthy in 1935. While I do not possess documentation of letters announcing their birth, I am sure their arrival must have been celebrated with joy and homage to Baba.

During Baba's first visit to Saidapet in 1930, Dastur, who I mentioned before was Baba's Secretary, was editing and publishing a monthly journal called Meher Message since 1929. To support the publication costs, Dastur was accepting non-spiritual, commercial advertisements from early 1930. Baba was appalled to see such banal advertisements in his ordained medium of spirituality. He must have had a few discussions about this, but Dastur was not convinced and needed the funds which were not forthcoming from other sources. So it continued. Finally after his Saidapet visit, Baba asked Grandpa to produce another quarterly journal called Meher Gazette with my Aunt as the editor, since Grandpa was in service. Both publications ran concurrently for two years. Meher Gazette was suspended from publication for a year in 1932 when

Grandpa undertook his European tour, but later resumed after Grandpa's retirement as a bi-monthly from April 1933, with Grandpa as editor. In the meantime, Baba relentlessly persisted to convince Dastur not to publish commercial advertisements in the Meher Message. This upset Dastur who did not oblige, especially when another publication was just commissioned. Finally, with Baba's directive, The Meher Message was discontinued with much protest from Dastur.

Dastur was known to my father who must have met him during one of his many visits. Around late 1933, Dastur visited Saidapet and met with my father and may have shared his disillusionment with Baba. Perhaps this was the final wedge in Father's association with the communal belief of all the other members of Meher Bhavan. After this meeting my father had firmly decided that he could not subscribe to Baba and so informed Mother. Since she was a staunch devotee, Mother must have taken this very hard leading to a serious fallout with Father. All alone in a house full of devoted followers, perhaps Father felt unwelcome to stay under the same roof as Grandpa. I recall loud discussions he had with Mother late at night that indicated he was not happy. This insurmountable rift resulted in Father leaving Mother and kids permanently and commencing his practice as a Licentiate Physician in a suburb called Chintadripet much north of Saidapet. Everyone at home was appalled and very upset. This had never happened before in Grandpa's family and was quite a scandal. So staunch was Mother's belief in Baba that she refused to leave "Meher Bhavan." But I learnt much later, she felt this was the only recourse for both Grandpa and Father. Leaving "Meher Bhavan" with her husband would mean that she would be abandoning Baba, so she stayed. There were no big fights or tearful farewells... Father just up and left one day and that was that. While Grandpa may have been very troubled by this event, he must have also seen the convoluted logic in this situation. To that end, he never bore any grudges nor did he prevent Mother or us to visit Father, which I recall we did a few times each month. Sadly, Father continued to be very sickly and aloof, so I never had the opportunity of getting to know him or even being with him much during my childhood. This void was filled by Grandpa whose resolve was that his grandchildren's future should not be jeopardized with familial discord. Father must have respected that and believed that Grandpa would be more focused in this effort. It is my belief that Grandpa and all of us were able to endure such harsh family disruptions due to our faith in Baba.

For ten whole years, Father never set foot in Saidapet, even for a visit. Then, Grandpa passed away during 1943 before the end of war as foretold by Baba. Somehow a year or so passed and I guess after much contemplation, Father came back to Meher Bhavan in 1944, for the first time in eleven years, to commiserate with Grandma and other members of the household. He did not know it, but this would be his last visit. As he was talking with Grandma, his Mother-in-Law, he clutched at his heart and appeared to be panting and short of breath. None of us even had time to react, and mere seconds later, he swooned over and stopped breathing. It was too late for the ambulance to come and when they did, they pronounced him dead resulting from a massive myocardial infarction. He was only forty seven then. Even now, I cannot fathom the import of this event. Why did he come back a year after Grandpa's demise? What happened to him while he was there? I can only ponder that perhaps Father had finally come to terms with his separation anxiety and laid rest his spirit.

I would like to pay homage to Grandpa and his cousin by giving an account of their sacrifice for the family. Grandpa was an institution by himself; kind, considerate and dedicated to family. He was a disciplinarian who wished his grandkids to be truthful and lead purposeful lives. I have never forgotten the norms he trained me in to deal with daily life. Some of them were:

- Never be in debt
- Be frugal
- Pray for happiness for the world and you'll get your share
- Be thrifty
- Get the savings habit
- Spend for what you need, not for what you want
- Obey rules
- Get the reading habit – enjoy books
- Exercise regularly

He found time to tell us to keep in mind phrases such as, "I am sorry", "I made a mistake", "Please forgive me", or "Thank you", "Take care", and "You are very kind". Also phrases like "Praise loudly, blame softly" and "Let there be no fungus, among us". He also regaled us with puzzles, word games, and the power of positive thinking, while he related historical anecdotes and stories. He shared such moments with us both at Bangalore and later at Madras.

When Grandpa admitted me at St Joseph's in Bangalore, summer of 1934, he also enrolled me, courtesy of Principal Rev Father C Browne, in the school's boy scout program. I opted for training in first aid, map reading and tent pitching during camp outings. I took to these activities with vigor and received many accolades. In Form III, during my second year, there was a grand Jamboree coinciding with the visit of the famed Lord Baden Powell, famed regent of the scout movement. I proudly participated in this event witnessed by Grandpa in the stands. Little did I know…this motivation by Grandpa would be the founding force in my future career and field activities.

I want to dwell for a bit on Grandpa's early days while in service which I gleaned in part from Grandma, long after Grandpa's demise in 1943. It was a revelation to learn of his sincerity in work, dedication to his duties, his sterling character as well as the trials, tribulations, financial losses and domestic upheavals he had to endure.

Being frugal in disposition, he saved some funds and deposited them in what I learnt was the reputed Arbuthnot Bank. I am not sure of the timeframe, but the bank declared insolvency due to bad loans, which spelled ruin for many families. I remember reading articles in "The Hindu", a leading newspaper in Madras, that overnight, many families became homeless. Some depositors became stark raving lunatics. I am sure he lost his savings, but Grandpa was stoic and weathered this debacle without as much as a mention.

When Grandpa married Grandma, he also wed into the joint family of the Saidapet residence, to be later named "Meher Bhavan", belonging to Grandpa's in-laws. His Father-in-Law, Raghavacharlu was the Tamil translator to Government in the rank of Chief Secretary. This was a highly acclaimed post. During this time, some ne'er do wells approached Raghavacharlu and showed some glistening specimens convincing him it was silver. In reality, it was actually Mica. They cajoled him to invest in the silver mining venture bonanza. He yielded in stages, each time investing more and more funds, ultimately borrowing large sums when his savings were all gone. The banks readily offered loans to Raghavacharlu due to his position, but this soon resulted in mounting debts. As the final salvo, the lure of the lucre being so empowering, Raghavacharlu pledged his Saidapet property as last resort collateral. Grandpa, in service away from home, was totally unaware of this until it was almost too late. When he was informed of this impending incident, he rushed to Saidapet while in service in the

Telugu Districts, and stopped the transaction from occurring. Knowing that Grandpa was in the legal profession, the charlatans quickly backed off and Grandpa managed to get back some investment from them which he used to redeem the property and offered it back to his Father-in-Law, debt free. Now his in-laws could live in their ancestral home for the rest of their lives.

Since Grandpa awakened to Baba in 1927, it was his staunch belief that almost a year after his meeting, Baba facilitated the rescue of the Saidapet house which was soon to be rededicated as "Meher Bhavan", in 1930.

Grandma told me that her father became quite ill and was bedridden during the early '30s. He began retaining water and his feet had become quite swollen, preventing him from moving about. But her mother, Pappammah, a diminutive but wiry lady, ever active and devoted to the family, took special care of her ailing husband. She had dedicated herself to Baba, having his *darshan* during his visits to "Meher Bhavan" in Madras and "Kamala Bhavan" in Bangalore. During this event, I recall an entry from Aunt Lakshmi's journal in February 1931 referring to Baba's miracle of healing the swollen feet of her Grandfather. Baba had sent by mail sacred ashes to be rubbed on Grandma's father's feet. When it was done, his feet miraculously regained their normal shape and he could move about. Whether it was faith that provided the healing or mystical powers of Baba, I will never know. The body is capable of things we cannot imagine under the power of faith and hope. But hope only comes from the recognition that someone or something that has touched God, is guiding us. I rest in this belief.

Grandpa was very reserved and kept to himself, so I used to seek Grandma's input to learn about events and personalities during his time. She told me the story of Grandpa's cousin, he, who joined Baba's *mandali* in 1937. Born 20th July, 1872, in Mysore City, Ramanujam's father, C.V.Rangacharlu was the personal assistant to the *Divan*[27] of Mysore. After his father's demise around 1875, his mother, originally from Madras returned with Ramanujam and two of his brothers, and settled in Madras amongst her relatives. Ramanjuam entered government service on 22nd July 1896 as a clerk at Teachers College in Saidapet. He advanced in his career by working hard, garnering several promotions and accolades, and retired from the Office of the Director of Public Instruction of Madras in 1927. In as much as he flourished in his career, he was empty in his heart and soul. He had a troubled family life with no domestic happiness and traveled all over India to places of religious importance, to seek solace. In his troubled state of mind, he prayed for an opportunity to meet a holy saint and offer his selfless service in return for spiritual bliss. It would appear his prayers were answered when he met Meher Baba, whom he termed "God, Guru, Father, Mother and my all". Upon, his *darshan* of Baba on March 1, 1930 at Meher Bhavan, he remarked "I met my God".

Since that time, Ramanujam was in constant correspondence with Baba. He accepted duties as treasurer, stayed at Meher Ashram cooking his own meals, assisting in keeping record of donations received, maintaining accounts in connection with running a night school for adults and feeding the poor and downtrodden. He spent his nights in contemplation of Sri Baba's image. He was asked by Baba to attend his birthday celebrations at Nasik, February 1937, which he did. Upon his return and meeting several spiritual leaders, he longed to be with Baba again, and wrote to him. At this time, Baba was in Rahuri, near Nasik, attending to *Mast*[28] work. These

27   Minister to the Maharaja
28   Spiritually intoxicated people

are people who have completely surrendered to God and have lost all sense of propriety. Many wander around improperly attired and incapable of supporting themselves. Unfortunately, many of the common folk regard this as a mental malady, or worse, a demonic possession and physically torment and ostracize them. The *Mad*[29] Ashram, which Baba founded, was a refuge for such devotees. Understanding Ramanujam's true desire, Baba wished for him to come and join him at once. This took place on 11th April, 1937. The telegram received from Baba stated:

STOP COME IMMEDIATELY STOP NASIK

After settling his affairs at Madras he joined his Master on 5th May, 1937 at Meherabad as a *mandali* member. He was attending to duties assigned to him at *Mad* Ashram, and assisting his other *mandali*, Pleader and Baidul. He also helped Adi Sr. during his trips to Madras in search of other *Mast* needing asylum. Acknowledging his devotion and selfless service to the cause, Baba nicknamed him as "Swamiji". Ramanujam kept a detailed journal and the last lines he wrote in his notes were, *"In my Master I fully realize that he is the embodiment of the Supreme Lord come to earth in human form. I offer my most humble prostrations to my beloved Master, Shri Sadguru Meher Baba, who will manifest himself as an Avatar."* His life with his Master enabled him to write a short booklet of poems entitled "At the feet of my Sadguru".

With Baba's permission Ramanujam stayed at Meher Ashram with Grandpa during his last days in 1941. Ramanujam had returned on 10th May, 1941 from his tour in South India where he had gone on Baba's Mission of Mercy and passed away quietly on 4th June, 1941 at Meher Ashram, repeating on his lips the sacred name of Baba.

---

29   Pronounced "Mudh" with a soft "d", and not to be confused with mad!

When informed of this unfortunate event, Baba sent the following telegram:

TO SAMPATH AIYANGAR STOP

NOBODY NEED FEEL SAD BUT RATHER GLAD BECAUSE RAMANUJAM HAS COME TO ME STOP

At various times since 23rd December, 1944, at Meherabad and other places, Baba lovingly remembered his departed followers. He kept a written list which included Grandpa and Swamiji entered as #12. Sampath Aiyangar - Circle Member of Madras and #13. Swamiji - Vedic pundit.

All during this time I recall vividly, following global events of the world at war. We heard that the prologue to the Second World War in Europe had commenced in the summer of 1939, when Adolf Hitler invaded Poland and continued his attack on the Russian front. England and France, the only allies at that time, opposed the annexation by Hitler, so Hitler turned his attention and invaded France. Italy under Mussolini joined forces with Nazi Germany and formed the "Axis of Evil" and the war extended to Northern Africa. The Axis countries were joined by Japan, now a naval might, and started occupying Malaysia, Philippines, and extended into Burma. Finally after being drawn into war after the attack on Pearl Harbor, USA joined the Allied Front and declared war on the Axis countries. I remember pondering why there was so much aggression in the world when clearly the chance for salvation as preached by Baba was not kill thy enemy, but embrace them. It was an enigmatic paradox to say the least.

Soon as we all came to experience, India, under British rule was threatened on several fronts with the Axis powers advancing towards Britain, France, and its colonies. Thus the "Raj" joined the war effort by sending its crack

"Gurkha" brigade as well as munitions[30] to aid the Allies in their war against the Axis powers. The threat to India from Japan since early 1942, led to the large scale evacuation of the eastern coastal states of India - the Coramandel coast, including the State of Madras. Strict blackout was enforced and air raid precautions were escalated to a war footing. These were terrifying times for our joint family. Grandpa was given responsibility of portions of south Madras where he took charge as Divisional Warden. Supplies were short at that time and he had to improvise. So trenches (fox holes) were dug in most areas and were covered by *palmyra*[31] leaf framework. He maintained regular drills where the residents of the area under his supervision were trained on first aid and emergency response, in case of an air raid from Japan along the eastern coast of India exposed to Burma and Malaysia.

Having occupied Burma, intelligence reports spoke of Japan's attacks on India by land forces deploying in Bengal via Burma and air raids along the Coramandel coast. I also heard a rumour that Japan had printed counterfeit Indian currency for circulation when it occupied India. I had heard about atrocities committed by the ruthless and mercenary Japanese army in Singapore and Malaysia. This was a very traumatic period and I remember conjuring up the image of Baba several times to preserve us all as often as I could. We prepared for the worst as best we could. Meher Ashram had its share of underground bunkers dug to the south of Baba's tree. The city was tense and was put on high alert. Except for the essential services, educational institutions and government offices were evacuated to makeshift locations within the interior districts which were considered safer. Rescue homes and correctional institutions at Madras shifted as well, nearly 200 miles inland.

---

30   Bangalores, named after the city, were very effective munitions deployed on Omaha
      beach in Normandie during the D-Day invasion
31   Indian Palm

For four long years since the attack on Pearl Harbour, Oahu, we feared the imminent subjugation of our homeland by Japanese forces. Ultimately, when Germany and Japan surrendered in 1945, the victory of the Allied forces and the reversal of fortunes for the Axis powers were hailed as a blessing by all of us.

CHAPTER Nine:

JOINT FAMILY

Grandpa had passed on in 1943 and Father in 1944. This was before I graduated from college with a BSc Honours degree. The only earning member at home, my Aunt, had to support the household expenses of our large joint family of five siblings, with four in school. The Elders decided to dispose of the Bangalore property which was being maintained by a friend-caretaker of Grandpa. This was no easy task as none of them was experienced in such transactions and there was a considerable delay in finding buyers. The Elders did not fully appreciate the real estate situation in Bangalore at that time. So my Aunt called a friend in Bangalore and beseeched her in desperation to sell the property at any price due to financial problems at home. Finally, a party interested in purchasing the property showed up and offered a ridiculously low price, just to test our desperation. Being in need of money and totally naïve about real estate negotiations, the Elders told the friend that the price was acceptable as is, and the property was sold under distress at the offered price with Grandma and Aunt present for the final sale. In a week, much to our surprise and dismay, my Aunt's friend relayed that the same property, was sold within days for three times the sale price offered to our family! We were surely taken in by a deceitful buyer, who was aware of our distress. While this would have been quite devastating, the Elders simply sought solace in Baba's words, "In life, you only get what you deserve." I refer to this incident not to illustrate that one should not work hard to realize their efforts...you create what you deserve in life as I have often found. I relate this to share the mindset of my Elders in their total acceptance that they got what Baba intended for them.

Being mindful and practicing Grandpa's principles of curtailing expenditure and living within our means, all of my siblings successfully completed their education earning graduate and post graduate degrees. The joint family had remained stable and financially solvent.

For quite some time, Grandma, Aunt, Mother and the rest of us had been earnestly requesting Baba for a *darshan* at Saidapet. Baba graciously accepted our humble invitation to meet and greet his devotees at Meher Bhavan and Meher Ashram, during April, 1947. Many may realize the significance of this date as the independence movement in India was at its highest intensity at this time. For this reason, the British had placed prohibitory orders and restrictions on public gatherings at functions to discourage freedom demonstrations. My Aunt convinced the authorities that there would be no public gathering, ceremonial welcomes or send offs and prohibitory orders would be strictly observed.

Baba's third visit to Madras was arranged for 2nd through 5th April, 1947. Baba accompanied by sixteen *mandali* arrived at Central Station Madras on the night of 2nd April. Aunt and Sister Vasumathi and a few devotees received Baba. The car bringing them to Meher Bhavan had Baba and Adi Sr, in front, while Aunt and Sister were in the rear. A strange drama took

Ref 14: Baba at Meher Ashram, Saidapet, Madras, taken on April 4, 1947

place early during this journey home. My sister somehow felt she should have had a chance to sit with Baba in front and so seemed somewhat unhappy and distant. Before the car could proceed a few yards, without so much as a word from my sister, Baba signaled the driver to stop the car, asked Adi Sr. to get in the rear and my sister to sit with him. She revealed later on to me that she felt ashamed to even have such selfish feelings... nevertheless, she was happy at the outcome. This was one of the many instances in our lives when we experienced that Baba sees all, knows all and is all. A quiet welcome ensued at Meher Bhavan when Baba arrived, followed by the *mandali* shortly thereafter. After *darshan*, Baba retired for the night.

On 3rd April, *darshan* commenced at around 8:30 AM in the decorated hall on the ground floor of Meher Bhavan. Baba had instructed us that he did not want devotees touching his feet or embracing him so, at the north eastern corner of the hall, we prepared a seat for him, decorated like a throne. Garlands and other offerings were to be placed at a lower level, near his feet. Although he would not have liked to be seen sitting in this royal position, he acquiesced noting that it would enable him to see things better. And also, this was what the devotees wanted and he did not want to disappoint them. By the end of the *darshan*, hundreds of devotees had his blessings moving in an orderly manner, faces beaming, some with eyes closed or tearful for the few seconds as they had their fill of Baba's smiling countenance. Between breaks Baba moved to Meher Ashram where he was seated on a pedestal under the very Peepul tree he had planted during his first visit on 2nd March 1930. It had now grown very large spreading its branches over the Ashram, shading it with a wide canopy of leaves. The tree appropriately symbolized the message that his devotees would find shelter and solace under his fold, just as under this huge tree. Two photos of Baba were taken and these were symbolic and prophetic in significance as we were to learn about much later[32]

A peculiar incident took place on 3rd April at the *darshan*. Among the huge gathering in the hall Baba saw an elderly gentleman with two younger men and gestured to Eruch, a *mandali*, to find out more about him. On Eruch's enquiry, one of the two youngsters accompanying the gentleman answered that the three of them had travelled by ship from Indonesia enroute to Mecca, to fulfill the Haj pilgrimage of their Grandfather. Madras was a transit halt for their ship which was to continue passage that night. During Haj one is supposed to maintain spiritual awareness; thus having heard that a spiritual master was giving *darshan*, they made their way to Saidapet. Through Eruch, Baba suggested if the elderly gentleman wished, he could perform the time honoured Muslim ritual of circumambulation as the token of Haj, in that very hall in the presence of Baba. The boys asked the Grandfather who willingly got up and did so thrice, to everyone's surprise. Baba's photo and literature were handed over to the group who left the hall. Why did Baba suggest this ritual, here in Saidapet? Why did the old man comply? This incident, while very mysterious, was to bear significance some thirty-eight years later...

The farewell message to his Madras devotees emphasized the supreme sweet word of love and concluded:

"I am always with you; still I have been happy for these few days that you have been with me. You may feel that I am now going away but you should never find that I have gone away. It is for you to hold on to me now and forever. On my part, my love and I will never leave you here or hereafter. May you be aware of it deeper and deeper; from day to day. My blessings to you all."

32   Ref 14

16- 4- 47.

Dear Kasthuri,

Shri Baba received your loving letter and He asks me to inform you that the contents of your letter made Him very happy. It made Him more happy to hear from you that you will always remember His advice and will do utmost to act accordingly.

Shri Baba wants you not to forget that He is always with you to help you in all your undertakings and He wants to be sure of His love and blessings for you.

Shri Baba has noted that Shrinathy and Jayanthy have done very well in the exams and He feels happy about it. Separate letters have been sent to them.

With love and blessings from Shri Baba.

yours fraternally
Elcha

Ref 15: Letter from Baba dated April 16, 1947 on his visit to "Meher Bhavan"

Baba and party left for Poona on the morning of 5th April of 1947 by the Bombay Express.

After Baba's momentous visit to Meher Bhavan, I had written a humble letter of thanks. The following is an extract from his reply[33]

16 - 4 - 47

Dear Kasthuri,

Shri Baba received your loving letter and he asked me to inform you that the contents of your letter made him very happy. It made him more happy to hear from you that you will always remember his advice and will do utmost to act accordingly.

Shri Baba wants you not to forget that he is always with you to help you in all your undertakings and he wants you to be sure of his love and blessings for you.

With love and blessings from Sri Baba

Yours Fraternally Eruch

That year, a significant event took place in the 3rd quarter of 1947. Independence from British rule was declared at last, at the stroke of midnight, August 14th. By this time I was on the Geology Department staff permanently. A gathering of staff and students of our department met at midnight of that very auspicious day and tearfully hoisted our National Flag, the *Tiranga*[34], and offered prayers for peace and prosperity for our Motherland. We paid homage to the freedom fighters

33   Ref 15
34   Tricolor, actually the name given to the Indian Flag

who relentlessly sacrificed their lives in the labor of this one ideal, and the numerous leaders facilitating this outcome who endured the hardship of prison.

After thirteen hundred years of foreign occupation, India had been liberated once and for all. *Vande Maataram*[35]!

---

35   "Homage to you O' Mother (land)"

CHAPTER Ten:

MEETING MY BELOVED

The following year, in 1948, there were some discreet events involving me and my job at Presidency College. As I had mentioned earlier, this college was the only institution offering Geology in the state system of education. A very prominent businessman and educationist, Dr Alagappa Chettiar, who later created the well known institution, AC Tech, had established a private Arts & Sciences College in Karaikudi, some two hundred miles from Madras. He was interested in initiating a BSc Geology program at this College under the affiliation of Madras University. This would earn the course accredited status and attract many students. He contacted my Professor at Presidency College to get his recommendation for an appropriate candidate to head the Department. To this end, my Professor, having already suggested my name to the Chettiar, went to great lengths to convince me to take the opportunity. While this was a very lucrative position, I had two concerns. Firstly, my new domicile would be far removed from Madras, and I would have to maintain two households with one salary. Secondly, what was being offered was not a tenured position, and I could lose my employment and income. It could be an adventure with a potential of fast career growth, but there were no guarantees. Could I take such risks being the sole breadwinner of my joint family? I was deeply perplexed. The offer was very attractive and flattering, but the risk was great. At this time, once again I sought Baba's wisdom and I realized what he had told me some time ago. He said "Do not become indifferent to your domestic responsibilities." Suddenly it became clear to me that I could not take this position in light of my enduring responsibilities to my Elders. I was also quite interested in continuing my research at Presidency College which had just been recently granted. Thus, I approached my Principal, Dr Abdul Haq, and requested him to kindly take my name out of consideration.

In retrospect, I am glad that I made that decision and was able to see my siblings and family prosper without any disruption of my employment or physical estrangement during this critical period of their development. Under the umbrella of Baba's guidance, cherished memories of Grandpa and assistance from Elders, I managed to perform my duties and progressed in my work.

Baba's blessings continued and manifested a turning point in my life during mid 1950. Since my high school days, while at Meher Bhavan, our family had good friends who were a great help to my Elders after Grandpa's demise. Once such was Mr. Natarajan, a teacher at the Christian College High School. Our family felt that Mr. Natarajan was a vital link chosen by Baba, as an amazing chain of events ensued culminating on 10th July, 1950, which was Baba's "Silence Day"[36]. It happened thus.

Since 1948, one Mr. Padmanabhan, was employed as the Assistant Executive Engineer during the early days of construction of the Hirakud Dam, a historic and remarkable feat of engineering in Orissa. Working

36   Baba entered into silence on 10th July 1925

under primitive conditions of housing and transport, the personnel were living in wartime era Lissen (Quonset) huts. Mr. Padmanabhan's family was not with him in those early days as his wife, Vedavalli, remained in Bangalore for she was sickly and bedridden. His eldest daughter Leela had terminated her education prematurely to be of help to her father, while relatives were tending to her ailing mother. Since she was approaching the age of marriage, proposals for her nuptials were being circulated amidst the *sashtris* [37] and Leela had to come to Madras during May to June of 1950 to stay with her Uncle. At this time her mother was being taken care of by Leela's aunt. One of her uncles was Mr. Natarajan's colleague, whom I mentioned earlier. When asked if he knew of any prospective grooms, Mr. Natarajan suggested to Leela's Uncle, information about my family. He advised a meeting of the two families to talk about a potential alliance between Leela and me.

Since it was an inquiry from Mr. Natarajan, a Baba devotee, my Elders were overjoyed knowing it was a sign from Baba. As was the usual procedure, horoscopic charts and photos were exchanged and the *shastri* pronounced that the alliance was cosmically quite sound. The next step was the actual meeting of both families which could become quite a spectacle. Traditionally such discussions and especially the meeting of the "boy" and "girl" would take place at the girl's Father's residence. But that was in Bangalore or Hirakud. Bangalore was not possible due to Leela's Mother's aliment and remoteness of the site at Hirakud would drive away any suitor! Since Leela was already in Madras, Mr. Natarajan and Leela's Uncle came to the rescue and suggested we meet there. So my Aunt, Mother and I accompanied by Mr. Natarajan went to Leela's Uncle's residence on the evening of 10th July, 1950. This was to be the place...this was to be the bride. I was too reserved and subdued to start the discussions. But under the hood, my cauldron was set on high and was brimming with concerns.

37   Matchmakers using astrology

How do you decide who to spend the rest of your life with, in such a short time? One way is to find out about the family history. This was best left to my Aunt and Mother who in a matter of minutes had laid out the entire genealogy of Leela's family and declared that the alliance would be well suited. I heaved a sigh of relief...one hurdle crossed. But, what of the bride to be? I had just seen her picture. But when she came in to the room and coyly sat down, I saw a vision and even began to wonder whether she would accept me. As always in my life, it was the grace of Baba that Leela accepted my hand that evening in marriage. We felt very grateful to Mr. Natarajan. Leela's father was informed about the successful event but I would see him much later as he could only obtain leave for the wedding.

I met my Father-in-Law when he came to Bangalore for the wedding, which was celebrated at their ancestral home in Bangalore, on 31th August, 1950. Soon after the wedding, we heard the good news that Mr. Padmanabhan, Leela's Father, was promoted to Executive Engineer. I surmised that not only did Baba have a hand in my nuptials, but propelled my Father-in-Law's advancement and illustrious career thereafter!

King's Road.
Ahmednagar
29-3-52

My dear Leela,

Baba received your letter of 23rd. You belonged to the Meher Baba family. You came to know of it later. Baba knows that he knew you were one of the family. You saw his pictures. You will see him in person. Then all the waiting will be recompensed.

Baba sends you his love and to all whom you love.

Yours brotherly,
Adi

Ref 16: Letter from Baba dated March 29, 1952 on the arrival of Leela into the fold

CHAPTER Eleven:

FATHERHOOD

When my marriage was announced, the Elders sent the invitation and proclamation to Baba. This is a Hindu tradition so that even if they may not attend, the recipient can bless the couple this way. Now Leela, my new wife, came to live at "Meher Bhavan" with a large joint family of my elders and siblings. Up to now, Leela was not aware of Baba or that he was our mentor. She had also never been part of such a large joint family. It must have been quite traumatic for her to move to a new city and live amongst a whole group of new people with very atypical yet, firm beliefs. I could just guess all the adjustments she would have had to make, but knew that she needed my full support. But then, I was gone most of the day for 6 days a week. Leela dedicated herself in taking care of the Elders and helping my siblings right away, without so much as a hesitation. It was hard work and I know my family must have been quite demanding. Slowly, Leela, mentored by Mother who introduced her to Baba, openly embraced his mission and beliefs. That was not enough.... she cherished a deep longing for Baba's *darshan*. Now it is sometimes said, if you have a passionate yen and it is a thing of faith, it can come true. This was evident when all at home received this mystical and unusual reply from Baba after receipt of her letter of March 1952[38]

Kings Road

Ahmednagar

29 - 3 - 52

My Dear Leela,

Baba received your letter of 23rd. You belong to the Meher Bhavan family. You came to know of it later. Baba knows you were one of the family. You saw his pictures. You will see him in person. Then all the waiting will be recompensed. Baba sends you his love and to all whom you love.

Yours Brotherly

Adi

It was like he knew all along that she would end up here, come into his fold and become part of his faith.

A couple of years passed when I received the blessed news that Leela was expecting around summer of 1953. She was at her Grandmother's residence at Bangalore by December 1952. It was a common practice for the expectant mother to go back to her family's house for the delivery. In the meantime, Baba's first tour of Andhra Pradesh, a coastal state north of Madras, took place in the new year, during January 1953. Mother had solicited Baba for his *darshan* during this tour. Sister Vasumathi was to accompany her. Baba's affirmative response included information for their

38 Ref 16

stay at Dr. Dhanapathy Rao's residence at Tadepalligudam, which was on Baba's tour itinerary. Mother and Sister were at Dr. Rao's residence from 17th January 1953 for the entire period Baba was there. Baba invited them to accompany his entourage during all of his visits. On January 19th, the day of the *darshan*, they met Baba and he enquired about everyone at Meher Bhavan. Then Mother conveyed the news of Leela expecting with a request to suggest a name for the baby. He suggested the name Meherdas for a boy and Meherkanthi for a girl, signifying the lotus flower which abounds in spiritual significance. As *Prasad*[39] for Leela and her baby, he gave a couple of pieces of bananas to be eaten by Leela and her baby, two flowers from a garland worn by Baba, and Baba's photo with a message.

On the morning of the 21st, Baba asked to see Mother and Sister before they left. He suggested they could travel with him in his car as they were going in the same direction for a while, before they needed to part ways. They were thrilled at this unexpected opportunity to be close to him. My Mother related the following events to me. As they traveled down the road, Baba called for an unscheduled halt at a place where the main road had a diversion. Then in a peculiar turn of events, Baba and his entourage got down and squat on one side of the main road. Nobody knew why he had stopped in this desolate section and why he was sitting on the road. Knowing Baba had his reasons, everyone waited for something to happen. Somewhat close to the diversion, Baba saw a tea shop (*bunk*) and asked Eruch to check with the owner if he had some cold soft drinks for the party. Meanwhile, the *bunk* owner had noticed the entire drama unfolding in front of his eyes and was a curious witness to the large gathering seated around a saintly person with reverence. Shortly, Eruch returned with a few drinks and went back to get more. An interesting feature of the soft drink glass bottles in those days was that, instead of a cap, there was a small marble lodged in the neck of the bottle, sealing the bottle. The marbles had to

39   Blessed mementos, sometimes edible

be pushed down, expertly, using a stopper or applying a very firm finger to release the aerated liquid before drinking. Needless to say, it was not an easy task. Eruch offered all the sealed bottles to Baba who distributed them to everyone. When everyone tried to dislodge the ball, they noticed that it had automatically pulled back issuing foam and ready to drink. Baba was smiling and then he asked Eruch to pay the *bunk* owner, who refused to accept payment in reverence to the holy person and his entourage. Baba convinced the owner to accept it as offering from an elder brother, who took the money reluctantly. As they were quenching their thirst, faint music was heard from the narrow country lane adjoining the main road. Soon, a group of dusty villagers – men, women and children, chanting *bhajans*, appeared. These devotees had known about Baba but were not fortunate to have a *darshan*. However, in spite of no advance publication of his itinerary, they somehow divined that he would be passing on this route, on this day and this time. They would certainly have missed Baba's *darshan* if he had not requested this unscheduled stop. . Whether he knew of their existence and desire is a mystery to me…I just believe that Baba does not turn away devotees. Baba has said, "I am not the slave of my lovers, but I am the slave of the love of my lovers". Soon after this unscheduled *darshan*, everyone boarded the cars and drove away. The place where Baba's party and Mother and Sister had to part came by the next day, and after a reluctant farewell, they journeyed to the Railway station for their return to "Meher Bhavan".

Upon their return to "Meher Bhavan" on 22nd January 53, Mother wrote a letter to Leela, who was in Bangalore, enclosing Baba's *Prasad* (offerings). To the joy of everyone, Leela delivered a healthy baby girl on 14th May, 1953 and promptly named her – Meherkanthi. Soon after, Leela wrote a letter to Baba announcing the birth and naming of her daughter. To which he replied[40]:

---

40   Ref 17

Aga Khan's Bungalow
Mahableshwar
(Dist Satara)
15th Dec 53

Dear Sister Leela,

Your very loving letter to Shri Baba was read to Him.

In reply to your Baba wants you to note that He knows well how much you and other dear ones at home think of Him. It is all due to your love for Him. But, Baba wants you all to love Him more so that the intensity of your love towards Him may make you realise how great and deep is this love for His lovers. Baba sends His love to you

Kasthuri and the dear little child.

Baba says that if He feels like visiting Meher Bhawan and if there is time on way to Andhra He might visit His place in Saidapet.

Baba wants you to convey His love to the dear old ladies of the house. By order of Baba

Yours fraternally

[signature]

पोस्ट कार्ड
केवल भारत में

INDIA

Srimati
Leela Kasthuri
नाम "Meher Bhawan"
पता 20 - Brahmin Street
डाकख़ाना Saidapet
ज़िला MADRAS - 15

Ref 17: Letter to Leela dated December 15, 1953 on the birth of Meherkanthi

Dear Sister Leela,

Your very loving letter to Sri Baba was read out to him. In reply to yours, Baba wants you to note that he knows well how much you and other dear ones at home think of him. It is all due to your love for him. But Baba wants you all to love him more so that the intensity of your love towards him may make you realize how great and deep is his love for his lovers.

Baba sends his love to you, Kasthuri and the dear little child. Baba says that if he feels like visiting Meher Bhavan, and there is time on his way to Andhra Pradesh, he might visit his place at Saidapet.

Baba wants you to convey his love to the dear old ladies of the house.

By order of Baba
Yours fraternally
Eruch

CHAPTER Twelve:

ONE "MISCHIEVOUS CHICKEN"

1954 was a momentous year for us at Meher Bhavan. For the first time since accepting Baba four years earlier, Leela had his *darshan* along with our ten month old child, Meherkanthi. It happened this way. Baba invited Mother, Leela, Meherkanthi and me to see him during March 1954. Baba was returning from his Andhra Pradesh tour and we met him enroute at Bezwada (Vijaywada) Station on the eve of March 4th. Little Meherkanthi had developed a fever that day and was restless throughout our journey. It was the beginning of summer in Madras and the heat was stifling, which made her even crankier. After travelling by two trains, we finally reached our destination which was the railway station waiting room at Bezwada. When it neared the arrival of his train, we hurried on to the railway platform and patiently waited for Baba's train. Finally, with a burst of steam, we saw it pull into the platform. We caught a glimpse of Baba's smiling face and waving palm, so we knew which carriage and compartment he was in. Mother and rest

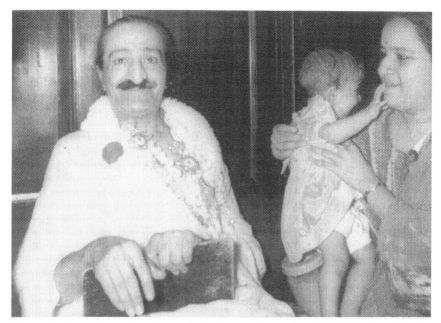

Ref 18: Baba with Meherkanthi, Leela and Mother, taken March 4, 1954, Bezwada Junction

Ref 19: "Mischievous Chicken" – drawn by Baba, while holding Meherkanthi's finger to the chalk.

of us boarded his carriage soon after it stopped. Baba was by himself. There was no one else in the compartment...what an opportunity!

Grandma had sent with us two containers of Baba's favorite sweet, *rava kesari*[41] prepared by her as our offering. We entered his compartment and paid our respects to him, after which we presented him the package from Grandma. He gleefully accepted this knowing very well what was in the container and while putting it away, Baba enquired about all of his faithful "Meher Bhavan" followers using his well known gestures. As advised by Mother we had taken with us a small slate board as well as a piece of chalk. This was the way Baba had grown accustomed to communicate after his vow of silence. Presenting the slate and chalk to him, Mother requested Baba to bless the child and initiate her into the three R's by using the slate and chalk piece. As he did for me, Baba got ready to perform this very traditional Hindu custom to instill the foundation for a good education. Of course, Meherkanthi, who had no bearing on the auspicious occasion remained still feverish, restless and somewhat surly. Baba, upon seeing this jokingly asked Mother if the baby really wanted this initiation. On Mother's respectful insistence, he took the child's hand and traced a rendering of his famed "mischievous chicken" sketch on the slate, the chalk's white color, contrasting in clear relief on the dark slate. Baba referred to himself as being the "mischievous chicken"[42] thus in essence, he represented himself rather playfully, to my daughter.

This seemingly ordinary event may be considered to have much greater significance years later, as it foretold Meherkanthi's future occupation as an educator. After achieving a Gold Medal in MA, Psychology, Meherkanthi started her career as a school teacher at Lawrence School, Lovedale and

---

41   Sweet made with Cream of Wheat and Saffron
42   In the book "The Nothing and the Everything", by Bhau Kalchuri, beloved Baba, describes *himself* as the "mischievous chicken".

Ref 20: Five Perfect Masters – gift to Meherkanthi

later branched into educating students with learning disabilities as well as counseling their parents.

Photos of Baba[43] with Meherkanthi and Leela as well as the slate marking were taken. All of us were thrilled and overjoyed with the visit. After a while, we felt that we had overstayed our welcome, so we conveyed our farewells and left the compartment. A few minutes later as we stepped down from the carriage, a virtual deluge of Baba's devotees poured into the carriage to visit him in his compartment. How lucky that we had him to ourselves all this time! As we made our way back to the Railway waiting room, we noticed that Meherkanthi was strangely calm and even smiling now. She was also no longer running a fever…

Later that night, we left by train to Madras. As soon as I got back and developed the pictures, I sent them with a letter of thanks to Baba. Three weeks after the *darshan* we received a letter from Baba's brother Jal *Bhai*, who thanked us for the photos taken at Bezwada station, which Baba had greatly appreciated. Baba then sent child Meherkanthi a telegram upon completion of her first birthday:

STOP MY LOVE AND BLESSINGS
TO YOU STOP BABA STOP

Separately, photographs of Baba were sent to Meherkanthi by his *mandali*. One was a unique matte of Baba and five Perfect Masters[44].

Over a year later, I received on 28th September, 1955, a special invitation from Adi Sr, marked "URGENT" from Kings Road, Ahmednagar. It was an announcement for a *sahavas*, a "gathering with the Masters", containing discourses and readings by Baba and his *mandali* as well as his Perfect

43   Refs 18, 19
44   Ref 20

Masters[45]. This was to be held at Meherabad, near Ahmednagar, in four sessions, comprising of about two hundred attendees per session. Each session would take seven days to complete. The *sahavasees* had to bear only their travelling expenses. Food, lodging, local transport and other expenses, would be shared among fifty of his select devotees. My session was set for the week of 11th November. My take away from this episode was that Baba makes the possible, impossible and the impossible, possible. Here is Baba's magic which has become the moral of my story:

Participation in the *sahavas* would require an absence of eight working days from my job. For any absence over 2 days I needed to apply for permission. The sanctioning authority for this unscheduled leave was the college Principal, who reviewed every application endorsed by the Head of Department, to whom I applied for eight days leave. I remember very clearly that unlike in any other situation, this time, I did not care to thank Baba for offering me this unique opportunity nor ask for his blessings so I could get leave. I was so sure my application would be granted that I did not feel the need to. The next day, I received a call to meet the Principal, which I noted, was rather unusual in the sanction of such a leave. Normally, he would have made his decision and sent the paperwork back to me. For the record, our Principal, Mr. Balakrishnan Nair, was a family friend having been a professor for my sister at the same college as well. He knew our family members were Baba devotees. He had also come home and was pleasantly surprised to see so many photos of Baba in our living room. So he knew the importance of this event to me and the opportunity I was being presented.

When I got to his office that day, he beckoned me to take a seat in front of him, and feigning ignorance asked me why I needed these eight days leave. In my request for leave I had laid out the entire program outline.

45   Those who guide him and enlightened him in his quest for salvation

Indulging his strange behaviour, I told him it was due to travel time from Madras by train to Meherabad and back with a couple of Sundays in between. He then asked me if I was going alone. I replied that my brother would be accompanying me. To my utter surprise, he then suggested that one of us, that is, my brother could attend on my behalf as well and thus I need not take leave! I was crushed and angry at the same time at this inane suggestion. But outwardly I maintained my calm and respectfully informed him that it was my earnest desire to go, as it was a unique and perhaps, once in a lifetime opportunity. Apparently, not appreciating such a rebuttal from a subordinate, and wanting to prevail, he stated that he was not inclined to sanction eight days in one stretch. To make it final, he added if I persisted in my request, he would refuse in record, noting "exigency of service" as a cause of refusal. That simply meant, he would put on file that I was an under achiever, thus the leave was refused. This was a low blow, but he had the power and the influence to permanently damage my record over such a minor issue. I promptly got up and left the office as there was nothing more to say. What hurt more not getting leave, was the blow to my ego. I lamented that the mistake was mine; in hindsight, perhaps I should have paid due respect to Baba, before pursuing this matter on my own. Nevertheless the matter was dead, and that was that.

When I returned to my desk, I promptly wrote to Adi Sr. that I would be unable to attend the *sahavas* as permission for leave was refused. Later that evening, when I told my brother about this, he too decided not to attend. He did not want to travel alone and also in deference to me. In a few days, I put this behind me and ploughed into my work. But would you believe it,...Baba would not let up. A week later, I received another invitation from him, to attend the last week of *sahavas*, this time in the last week in November. Only in reverence to Baba, and for no other reason, I sent in another leave application for eight days, thanked Baba for this opportunity knowing full well, that this too, would be declined. After I handed in the application duly approved by my Department Head at the Principal's office, I promptly forgot about it. This time, there were no calls asking me to visit the Principal's office. The next day, as I entered my office after the morning lecture, there was my request form, neatly placed in the middle of my desk. Knowing the outcome, as I picked it up to toss it in the waste bin, I chanced to glance at the approval box on a curious whim, and to my surprise, Mr. Nair had signed his approval! Did he have a change of heart, was he just playing with me all this time...or was this Baba's way of saying, *you give me impossible, I make it possible*? Thrilled with this turn of event, that night Brother and I immediately sent our ebullient acceptance reply to Adi Sr. In the weeks between this response and our departure, I received blessed news again, which I imagine, was the real purpose of this beckoning from Baba. Leela, on October 28th, 1955, conveyed that she was expecting again. I was overjoyed to learn that I would become a father once again by mid next year, and decided that since my trip would happen well in advance, I would take some baby clothes given to me by Mother to be blessed by Baba.

Mehernath, and I arrived at Dhond, on 27th November 1955. By then the weather had cooled down considerably, and it was very pleasant. The Ashram, which was within driving distance had arranged transport which took us to Meherabad, directly by that evening. Surprisingly comfortable and cozy tent lodgings and boarding facilities were provided for all of us. As I looked around I could sense a vibration of spiritualism in the air. Imagine, all these spiritual masters and "awakened" devotees... all in one place! Due to a few cancellations, sessions were combined and the final session had burgeoned to include about four hundred attendees, twice the normal size. The five day *sahavas* commenced with Baba's *darshan* on the morning of the 28th. In the afternoon, Brother and I had the privilege of a private audience with Baba in his cabin. Eruch, Adi Sr. and Jal were also asked to be present. After all of us paid our respects and took our seat, Baba said that Eruch had read and conveyed all our letters to him from "Meher Bhavan" that morning. Baba was very pleased with our achievements and said he knew we all loved him very much. Then referring to Grandma, he said she would keep chanting his name as a source of support, right up to her end. After a few additional words, Brother and I got up and presented to Baba the sweets he always cherished and the baby clothing of my expected second child for his blessings. After the ritual, we collected the clothing and *Prasad* offered by him consisting of fruit and flowers to be given to Leela as before. We then asked him if he could ordain another *sahavas* at Meher Bhavan. He replied that he would consider this. I then asked him to suggest a name for my soon to be born child. Baba stated that it was not time yet, and he would inform us later. I was puzzled but perhaps there was an auspicious time for this in Baba's mind. Sadly, it was time for us to leave and Baba embraced both of us and wished us safe journeys... but not without an opportunity to record this event. A photo of me and my brother with Baba was taken to commemorate this significant occasion[46]. Soon after the completion of the event, Brother and I left Meherabad and arrived at Meher Bhavan in time for me to join work.

---

46   Ref 21

Ref 21: Brother and I with Baba at *sahavas*, November 28, 1955. Author on far right

CHAPTER Thirteen:

TWO "MISCHIEVOUS CHICKENS"

By May of '56, all of us were anxiously awaiting Leela's second delivery. Our physician, Dr. Rangachari, living on the same street was a personal family friend and had attended to generations of "Meher Bhavan" residents. He regularly attended to Leela making sure there would be no complications and projected normal delivery towards end of May or early June of 1956. As predicted, on the 5th of June, Leela had a safe delivery and my second daughter was born into the fold. This time, as we had already sought Baba's input, it was Mother's idea to name her granddaughter Nirupkanthi, "formless lotus", as she visualized the alphabetical sequence, K (Kasthuri) L (Leela), M (Meherkanthi), and now, N (Nirupkanthi). This way, the naming system was perpetuated and her name had "kanthi" signifying the lotus, which was the same suggested by Baba to her older sister. Clothes blessed by Baba that I collected during the *Sahavas* event of last year, were draped over the baby in a time honoured tradition. To this day, for some reason, I cannot recollect, nor do I have any record, of the events that immediately ensued. I don't know if I communicated with Baba, but I am sure that Mother would have informed him about my second daughter's birth. Also there may have been responses from Baba about this event or of my wedding in 1950, neither of which I possess. Leela has filled in the blanks as she has continued doing so into my later years. Nirupkanthi grew up a cheerful and content child and did not crave much attention. It's almost like...she was just happy to be there.

Going back in time a couple of years, right after our *darshan* of Baba at Bezwada station in 1954, Baba had graciously invited Mother and family to come see him again at Guru Prasad, Poona. This would be Mother's very first visit to the ashram. We requested Baba's *darshan* based on this invite, and it was granted during December 1957. Accordingly Mother, my sisters, Leela, my daughters and I went to Poona on 8th December. Nirupkanthi was eighteen months old at that time. This was the very first time also for the whole family to be travelling together and promised to be a memorable trip. With time on hand, reservations for everyone were made on the Western Railway link to Poona. The trip would take two days and one night passing through some of the most rugged and beautiful *ghat*[47] sections of Indian Railway.

Mother had dedicated herself to Baba at her very first sight since she met him in 1930. Her staunch and indisputable devotion to Baba was rare and she considered that as his gift to her. Trials and tribulations in her life only deepened her love and faith. Baba knew this through the unspoken word, and stated that her faith in him was very strong. She transmitted this gift to her children and her grandchildren. "She was the bravest of Baba's Meher Bhavan family", remembered Adi Sr. It was this which had drawn her to Baba and his interest in calling her to Poona.

---

47   Mountainous

Ref 22: Postcard from Baba for Nirupkanthi, March 2, 1963

After reaching Poona we were taken to Guru Prasad and immediately had Baba's *darshan*. All of us once again paid our respects and Baba was overjoyed to see generations of his followers, each one "awakening" those younger to them. After Mother had presented him once again, the special sweets prepared by Grandma, just as in Bezwada in 1954, she requested Baba for a favor. She had brought with her, in a bag, a slate board and a piece of chalk. She requested Baba to initiate her second granddaughter Nirupkanthi into the 3 R's, just as he had done with her sister. Somehow, when she took out the slate board, the chalk piece had gone missing. Anxiously, she looked everywhere for it but it was not to be found. She did not know if this was an omen and worried about her young granddaughter's future. Was she not entitled to be blessed? Sensing her troubled mind and without hesitation, Baba smiled, and asked Eruch to fetch a piece of marble stone from out in the courtyard. Upon procuring it, he held the baby's tiny hand and guided it to trace Nirupkanthi's blessing. It was once again, the well known tracing of himself as the "mischievous chicken". Only this time the drawing was but faintly visible as the stone did not contrast as well as a chalk with the slate. Nevertheless the event ensued without much ado and after taking our blessings we took leave of Baba. We stayed in Poona for a few days as we enjoyed the cool December weather in Poona before returning by rail to Madras a week later.

I cannot but ponder the significance of the event of Nirupkanthi's initiation. Was it just an inconsequential quirk of fate or did it have a hidden message? In reflection, I surmise that using of the stone and the slate, however insignificant at that time, perhaps foretold my second daughter's occupation as an Architect several years into her future. Nirupkanthi completed her BArch course and as part of her internship in 1977, she reconstructed the

Parsi graveyard at Ootacamund whose caretakers were followers of Meher Baba.

The years went by as did many *darshans* of Baba, and when Nirupkanthi was in Class II B at Church Park Convent, she received a postcard[48] which was sent by Baba to her on 2nd March, 1963. We continued to grasp every opportunity to visit Baba and at many such occasions he would regale us with stories of his past, voicing his anecdotes as always through Eruch, his interpreter.

---

48   Ref 22

Ahmednagar   Aug.28, 1963

Sri A. K. Kasthuri
c/o Sundar Lodge
Cherry Rd.
Salem 7 (Madras State)

My Dear Kasthuri,

It was a pleasure to receive your reverential and
loving letter to beloved Baba of the 21st.

Perhaps you are aware that on His return from Poona
after His summer stay there of three months, Baba has
again retired in seclusion and is not seeing or meeting
anyone. Only correspondence relating to His work is
being received and sent to Him for information. I however
sent your letter to Him, as it was addressed to Him,
and you will be pleased to know that it was read out
to Him.

Baba wants me to convey His Love - Blessing to you.

I am happy to find you so upright and honest in your
duties and so conscientious in your behaviour. My prayer
to Baba is that you and all dear Janaky's children, may
propser with a detached outlook on life and continuous
remembrance of Baba.

With loving regards to you and yours,

Yours brotherly,

Adi K. Irani

Ref 23: Letter from Baba on my promotion and new assignment, July 1963

CHAPTER Fourteen:

HEAVENLY CALLS

In July 1963, I was offered a promotion to the position of full Professor within the State Education Department. This position however, was to be located at the Government College within the system, in the town of Salem, some 150 miles southwest of Madras. This promotion did not come with a significant increase in wages and I still had to support a large, aging joint family with small children, as well as two domiciles. Yet, this time, I decided to accept this position as it was within the service and an opportunity to rise professionally within this system. The position was tenured and I could come back to Madras with much better prospects. I had to make a very quick decision and was only given a day to make up my mind. I contemplated on Baba and took this challenge considering it as a gift from Baba who was presenting me with another opportunity to advance myself since I declined the last one in the interest of supporting the joint family. I was relieved from Presidency College, Madras and joined duty at Salem within a day of the promotion as was the general policy. The Geology course students, twenty-four in number, had already been admitted as the college had reopened in June. I wrote a letter to Baba about this promotion and transfer. Baba's reply was to my Salem address[49]. I was happy to get Baba's blessing on this new assignment conveyed to me through Adi Sr. as it confirmed that I had made the right decision.

While I was away at Salem from 1963 onwards, Leela stayed at Meher Bhavan attending to the Elders. Her dedication in taking care of the household, Elders, peers and my daughters was commendable….and she did it all by herself. By this time both my girls were studying at the renowned Church Park convent, Madras, starting 1957. I missed being with them, but desire in providing an uninterrupted education to her daughters motivated Leela to stay back at "Meher Bhavan." She had active cooperation and help from Elders in the family and had soon become Mother's pet. Leela at times has mentioned to me that Mother alone truly understood what she was all about.

Grandma, since 1964, was losing her eyesight and Leela, also Grandma's favorite, was a solace and caretaker for her. So attending to the Elders and my younger siblings and girls became her full time job. During vacations, I would return to "Meher Bhavan" to be with family for a few days as often as I could. Coming back brought me peace and prepared me for the next term of temporary bachelorhood. But what was most joyful was that during school vacations, Leela and the girls would come to Salem for a short visit. I began to look forward to that more than anything else. At every opportunity I got, I took it upon myself to continue the legacy of Grandpa and coach my girls of the lessons learnt. I also encouraged them to understand the bliss that was Baba, and lay their faith upon him. I did not compel nor deploy any strict measures in my instruction. Just by speaking of my experiences of joyful memories and hardships, my girls soon began to understand my lifelong mission…make this life meaningful… cherish it, as it is your gift from God.

49   Ref 23

The years just seemed to melt away and soon I returned to "Meher Bhavan", yet again, for summer vacation in early April 1966. I was to stay there through the first week of June. Grandma was slowly declining in health, although she was not bedridden. I could see that every task she had to do was laborious for her. Still, her mind was sharp as a tack. As with every time I came on vacation, she would insist I return as soon as possible so I would not miss my work. She was always fond of me, which I remember vividly, as I was mostly with her all my life.

That early May, Vasumathi, who was in Bombay working for Lever Bros at this time invited Leela and our girls to vacation with her so Leela could get some respite from taking care of Grandma. Leela was initially reluctant, but Grandma insisted Leela and the girls go and not worry about her. Additionally, Vasumathi had sent all of them air tickets and they all travelled by air for the first time in their lives!

Leela and the girls were having a fabulous vacation but during their absence, Grandma took ill suddenly on the morning of 30th May, 1966 and was having trouble breathing. Our family doctor told us that fluid was slowly entering and filling her lungs and that could not be healed at her age. We knew her end was near. As usual, Grandma insisted that I needed to be getting back to work at Salem. In her condition, I could do nothing but lie to her that I would be leaving the next day. In fact by this time, I had already missed my reservation and had to postpone my return by a couple of weeks. On that critical day, neither I nor my brother had left her bedside since dawn. Even through our tired and sleepy eyes, we could note that while seemingly asleep, unconsciously her lips were moving, uttering silently, Baba, Baba, Baba. Like a flash, both of us simultaneously recalled Baba telling us nearly a decade ago, during the Meherabad *sahavas,* that this would happen. It was a melancholy and yet a symbolic experience for us to see this prophecy come true signifying the imminent passage of my beloved Grandma. She uttered Baba's name till the late evening for over 12 hours, until her mouth suddenly went still indicating that she was with us no more. She must have waited for Leela, but unfortunately, her favorite could not be by her side. Even with air travel it was not possible, and both Leela and my sister came back a few days later with the girls when we informed them of Grandma's demise. I remember the deep sorrow and remorse I was experiencing over the next few days. Grandma had been by my side from the very time I began to crawl and it was like a part of me was gone forever. With tearful eyes as the eldest male in the household, I completed the final rites witnessing the end of an era of both my primary caregivers passing on.

I returned to Salem shortly and worked in earnest to put my sadness behind me. My work was progressing well but the Geology department was started without a library or any Geological specimens necessary for the courses. These were steadily acquired in stages after funds were allotted. The first batch of twenty four students appeared for their BSc Geology degree exams during May 1966. The great handicap with this first batch was that most of their teaching materials were received only at the end of the second year of their three year course. To make up for the lack of such materials and not to let the students fall back in comparison to the other institutions, our dedicated teaching staff and support staff worked as a team arduously and developed their own teaching guides. This paid off, as our first batch of students achieved 100% passing grades and captured the first position as an institution in the University system of colleges.

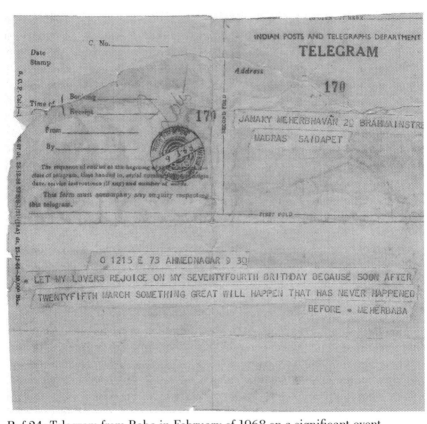

Ref 24: Telegram from Baba in February of 1968 on a significant event

Back in "Meher Bhavan" around early February of '68, Mother, Janaky, received a telegram from Ahmednagar which read thus[50]:

STOP LET MY LOVERS REJOICE ON MY SEVENTY FOURTH BIRTHDAY BECAUSE SOON AFTER TWENTYFIFTH MARCH SOMETHING GREAT WILL HAPPEN THAT HAS NEVER HAPPENED BEFORE STOP MEHER BABA STOP

When Mother informed me of this, I puzzled over what this portended. I guessed I would have to wait till March twenty-fifth.

Very soon after, while at Salem, I received a phone call in the evening that Mother took ill suddenly and was in a coma. Saying prayers to Baba, I applied for a few days leave and reached "Meher Bhavan", the next morning. Mother was still in a coma. Our family doctor could not say what was likely to happen, unless she showed any response. I had booked for my return to Salem for 12th February, but was hesitant to leave Mother. So I applied for and received a month's paid leave and stayed back. Amazingly, she recovered suddenly on this day, recognized every one of us, was surprised to see me and asked why I was at "Meher Bhavan". Our family doctor, though surprised, felt that she had recovered. Once again, I felt that it was the magic of Baba keeping her alive. All of us rejoiced and offered homage to Baba…but our joy was short lived. Shockingly, she stopped breathing on the morning of 15th February. Only a few hours earlier, she had spoken to my Aunt and asked her to go to work and not worry about her. Our family doctor came and after examining her, hurried home without a word. He knew it was over. When we found her still, all of us were grief stricken. My Aunt rushed home when told of the passing of her younger sister. Baba was informed by telegram and the following two replies by telegram to my Aunt and Sister were received on 16th February 1968[51]:

50   Ref 24
51   Ref 25

INDIAN POSTS AND TELEGRAMHS DEPARTMENT

TELEGRAM

L 32

199

Time of { Booking
Receipt

From

By

The sequence of entries at the begin
class of telegram, time handed in, serial number
date, service instructions (if any) and number of words.

This form must accompany any enquiry respecting
this telegram.

Address 199

VASUMATI MEHEREBHAVAN 20

BRAHMAN STREET MADRAS SAIDAP

16-2-59

0 1715   E 37   AHMEDANAGAR   16 32

MY DEAR JANAKAY HAS COME TO ME FOR ETERNAL REST IN MY

BLISS SHE IS BLESSED MY LOVE BLESSING TO YOU LAKSHMI AND

JANAKYPRAIVAR === MEHERBABA INSECLUSION =====

Ref 25: Telegram from Baba to Sister

To Aunt

STOP YOUR TELEGRAM STOP VASUMATHIS PHONE
CONVEYED TO BABA STOP FROM HIS DEEP SECLUSION
AVATAR MEHER BABA GIVES HIS LOVE BLESSING TO
SISTER JANAKY AND BABA SAYS JANAKY IS VERY
DEAR AND IS CLOSE TO HIM STOP BABA WANTS
JANAKY FAMILY TO REMEMBER HIM AND TO REMAIN
RESIGNED TO HIS DIVINE WILL STOP BABA SENDS
HIS LOVE TO YOU VASUMATHI AND JANAKY PARIVAR
STOP ERUCH STOP

To Sister

STOP MY DEAR JANAKY HAS COME TO ME FOR
ETERNAL REST IN MY BLISS STOP SHE IS BLESSED
STOP MY LOVE BLESSING TO LAKSHMI AND JANAKY
PARIVAR STOP MEHER BABA IN SECLUSION STOP

While Grandpa and Grandma initiated my belief in Baba, it was Mother who fanned the flames of my deep absorption of his teachings and mystique. She was solely responsible for keeping our faith alive in him. By constant correspondence with Chanji and later with Adi Sr., she had amassed almost every photograph of Baba, captioned with date. She meticulously arranged these in several albums, along with her rich collection of Baba literature. Also, beloved Baba gifted her the *padukas*[52] which he wore during his Meher Bhavan visit in 1947. Baba followers commonly presume this special gift signified that all surviving members are dedicated to him and pray to receive his blessings. Thus it is revered as such. My sisters carefully catalogued these articles and placed the sacred *padukas* at "Meher Ashram" for all to see and pay their respects.

---

52 Footwear: It is common Hindu custom to worship the footwear worn by enlightened people

It was heart wrenching for me to head back but I joined duty at Salem on 8th March 1968 and just immersed myself in my work yet again. I should mention by this time, the Congress Party in Madras, which had been in power since independence, had been completely routed. A new government promoting the Dravidian Tamil culture had come into power with an inspired and energetic Chief Minister, Mr. Annadurai. Madras would change forever. Soon, in due respect to Tamil heritage, the State of Madras was renamed Tamil Nadu: Land of the Tamils. In the coming millennium, the city of Madras, which derived its name from Madrasipattanam, and shortened thus by the British Raj, would be renamed "Chennai".

In April 1968, the African American Civil Rights Leader and winner of the 1964 Nobel Peace Prize, Dr. Martin Luther King was assassinated in Memphis Tennessee, USA. I wondered...is this what Baba foretold in his telegram of Feb 1968? But he said ...*something great will happen that has never happened before*...how could this tragedy be great? But then I remembered, life and death to Baba were, but mere page markers in time; he was referring to the significance... The significance, that achieving civil rights and liberties for all races, castes and creed was but the penultimate mission for humanity. Something for which Rev. Martin Luther King had sacrificed his life. Something his death had inspired in the world: *put hate aside and embrace the gift of life.*

On quite another note, four days later, North Vietnam agreed to peace talks with USA. Eventually this led to the end of the conflict in Vietnam.

In 1967, as I had mentioned, sanctions for educational materials were lagging over a year behind. So also was the sanction of funds for conducting field work which was a critical part of the study of Geology. During the academic year 1968 - 69 we received this sanction for the field work from the previous year. The first ever field work for the Salem institution was undertaken for a week's duration during January 1969. This was a great opportunity for me to cope with my losses and immerse myself on a road trip, teaching eager young minds of the wealth of knowledge lying beneath their very footsteps. I was gone for a period over two weeks and during this time; we were virtually cut off from all communications since we were in very rural and underdeveloped areas.

One day, while we were at our first camp, one of my students had purchased a local newspaper. Seeing it in his hand, I asked if he would let me read it after him. Out of respect, he handed it to me immediately stating that I could read it first. I rose to receive it and driven by the thirst for finding out what was going on in the world, I quickly glanced through the pages in search of an interesting article. The newspaper was dated the February 1, 1969. In the national section towards the middle of the paper was an article that took my breath away. I became weak in my knees and had to sit down, trying to quell my overwhelming sorrow as I read and re-read the same lines, over and over again, in the hope that my eyes were deceiving me. The single line read: On January 31st, the renowned spiritual master, Avatar Meher Baba, shed his mortal body and passed on into the spiritual world. I wanted to scream out in the pain of loss. Why were all the ones close to me leaving me? Over the span of three years, I had lost my parent, my guide and my spiritual mentor. One part of me just wanted to end the field trip and rush back to "Meher Bhavan" to commiserate my sorrow. Another part of me, which perhaps was guided by Baba's spirit, told me to respond to the call of duty. The second part prevailed and the field trip went off as planned. When I came back, I tried, but since it was not a family emergency, I could not get leave to visit my family at this juncture. We were in our final term of courses for the academic year and I could only be with my family during the summer break. I continued on with my tasks meticulously. When I had a quiet moment I pondered... Meherkanthi would be completing her High School in March 1969 while Nirupkanthi would be taking her annual exam for the III form (Eighth Grade) at the same time. These thoughts of life moving on and rejoicing in my children's achievements helped me cope with completing the term.

I thought that Baba's influence upon me and my life was over. Of course, I would keep him alive in my memories and faith, but how could the Master respond to my needs again? I was indeed proven wrong. Those that walk upon this earth with a spirit larger than their body are not part of *samskara:* the life-death cycle. They live on and have their influence wherever they are, in whatever form. While I was at Salem, during early 1969, I learnt that Aunt had been praying to Baba that I could somehow manage to return to Presidency College, Madras after a six year hiatus from "Meher Bhavan." While this was my earnest dream as well, there was no position suitable of my seniority available through that time. But Aunt was relentless in her belief that Baba's influence would once again prevail. One day in March of '69, she received an unsolicited call from a friend of hers at the education department of the government. The friend called to inform her that for the first time, a post of Additional Professor was created at Presidency College in four departments including one in Geology. This was announced officially a few weeks after. My Aunt phoned me bursting with excitement, asking me to submit a request for transfer immediately. I did not want to seem too eager and decided that I would just contemplate upon Baba and let him do his will. I shivered with excitement in the thought that there was a chance of ending my hiatus and returning as a full professor to Presidency College and once again living amongst my loved ones. I suffered in silence for over three long months, praying every day for the impossible. On July 4th, on my way to Lecture, an office courier handed me a registered letter in a large brown, recently opened, envelope. The Sender stamp stated: Tamil Nadu Department of Education. The addressee stamp stated: To be opened by addressee only – confidential and urgent. I also noticed it was addressed to the Principal who had apparently reviewed the contents, and had marked on it in pen...forward to Prof. A.K.Kasthuri. I was so nervous to see what was in it so I put it amongst my lecture materials and proceeded to class. I don't remember a word of what I taught that hour and I do hope my students forgive me for this, but my mind was truly elsewhere. Upon the completion of the session, I rushed back to my office and after saying a prayer to Baba, with trembling hands, I pulled out the single sheet of paper in the open envelope and just read the one line displayed under the salutations:

Effective immediately, Prof. A.K.Kasthuri is appointed to the position of Additional Professor of Geology, Presidency College, Madras. He is to join duty as of July 7, 1969

I could not believe my eyes. I read it about a dozen times; then I read it again. I went to my Principal and discussed the letter with him. He said he had been contacted by HQ and the letter was genuine. When asked about me, my Principal said to the official contacting him that while he would certainly find it difficult to fill the void, he was happy to see such an advancement coming to someone so deserving. Almost shedding a tear, I thanked him profusely and after coming back to my office immediately informed Leela and my aunt. They were delirious with joy as I had created quite a ruckus in their humdrum routine. I told Leela not to tell the girls as I wanted to do that myself and I quickly packed my belongings and left Salem College, for the last time as an educator. I could not but marvel at this fact: I miraculously received this transfer order in July, 1969, and the college had already reopened in June. This was unprecedented, but of course, not in my case. Baba had seen to that time and time again in my life, and perhaps in years yet to come. I made a solemn prayer to Baba for his bounty.

Receiving my transfer order on a Saturday, I left immediately as my order was to join forthwith at Presidency College, 7th July, 1969, the following Monday.

The homecoming reunion with family brought back a flood of memories and a lot had happened during my absence from Meher Bhavan. Since I left home in 1963, Grandma had passed on in 1966 and Mother in '68. My Aunt was my anchor and Leela dedicated herself to our joint family and our girls' education.

'Tis true, life is full of joy and sorrow. You cannot have one without the other. People enter this world and depart; that is a constant. We strive to imbibe their experience and tutelage and hope to become better people. While it is hard to let them go, we also need to know that they too are on this earth for a reason. When time comes and their work is done here, we have to imagine that they are leaving to fulfill other tasks that are beyond this earthly world. But we can celebrate the fact that what they did in this world will help them earn a better place in the cosmos, and that should bring us peace. Family to me is so precious and most underrated today. People yearn for achievement or accolades to satisfy their own sense of self esteem and station in society. Many times they forget the hidden wealth that is presented to them in the form of family. To serve this family, cherish their loving memories, protect them from harm's way and help them understand their true mission on this planet, have remained my focus. Added to that, to be among the few who have had the gift of facing life guided by Avatar...well, needless to say, I feel that I have been blessed with immeasurable wealth.

Much later in my life during December 1985, Leela, Meherkanthi's son, Siddharth and I were on a pilgrimage to Meherabad. This time when we met Eruch, our discussions lead to the mysterious and unexplained events that always seemed to abound when we were around Baba. One such event had occurred some thirty eight years ago in early April of 1947. In this event, Baba was once again gracing his devotees at Meher Bhavan. At this time he had curiously asked an old man, accompanied by his two grandsons enroute from Indonesia and on his way to Mecca, to circumambulate him in reverence to the Muslim tradition at Haj. We all had found that strange, but knew Baba had a reason. Now after thirty eight years, we learnt of his mystique. Eruch mentioned that after several years, he received a letter from Indonesia that had presumably been lost as it had been postmarked May of 1947. In this letter, one of the grandson's accompanying the old man to Haj wrote:

"My grandfather never reached Mecca. He died enroute and so we brought him back home. His dying words were, I have completed my quest. In Baba, I have received salvation. Our family conveys our thanks and gratitude for the opportunity of Baba's darshan and for this spiritual awakening."

My body tingled when I heard this as I knew that Baba, the all knowing, had once again showered his compassion upon an unknowing devotee.

There have been several challenges, hurdles and tough decisions in the ensuing decades, but solutions always found their way to me one way or another, miraculously and unsolicited. Even after Baba left his earthly body in 1969, to this day, I feel he is eternally looking after me.

Jai Baba!

Epilogue:

More than twenty years after the demise of my beloved Baba, my grandson, Nirupkanthi's son, Vikram, then four, playfully referred to Baba as "Baba Thai". *Thai* in Tamil refers to Mother. All these years my concept of Baba was that he was my father figure. During mid 2000's I read an account from Baba literature where he had said that only, during this incarnation, he has come as Baba the mother as well as Baba the father. Thus my grandson innocently awakened this significance at my late stage in life. I believe it was a divination to emphasize what I had missed in life. This once again reaffirms my faith that the avatar of Baba is eternal.

The saga continues….

P.S.: In addition to the letters and photos in this narration, more correspondence from Baba, his *mandali* and Baba groups, as also and extensive photo record of events, have been preserved carefully. These include documents past January 1969 right up until present day.